THREE CLASSIC DON JUAN PLAYS

TIRSO DE MOLINA

The Playboy of Seville, or Supper with a Statue

Translated by Adrienne Schizzano Mandel and Oscar Mandel

MOLIÈRE

Don John; or, The Libertine

Translated by John Ozell
Revised and augmented by Oscar Mandel

LORENZO DA PONTE

The Punished Libertine, or Don Giovanni

Translated by Adrienne Schizzano Mandel and Oscar Mandel

THREE CLASSIC
DON JUAN PLAYS

Edited with an introduction

by

OSCAR MANDEL

UNIVERSITY OF NEBRASKA PRESS · LINCOLN

First Bison Book edition: September 1971

Contents

Introduction

The man who created Don Juan was a monk and dramatist of the first half of the seventeenth century, Gabriel Téllez, better known as Tirso de Molina, and considered today one of the four best playwrights of Spain's Golden Age.[1] In 1630 a play entitled *El Burlador de Sevilla y convidado de piedra* (*The Jester of Seville and the Stone Guest*) appeared under his name in a collection of works by Lope de Vega "and other authors." It is virtually certain, however, that Tirso wrote the play in the period between 1612 and 1616.

Nothing in his own life or in contemporary documents indicates that he or Spain was aware that a "universal myth" rivaling that of Faust had been created. The *comedia* may have been a success—the evidence is of the scantest—but Tirso himself failed to include it in the five volumes of his plays whose publication he supervised. The matter of the play caught on while Tirso was still alive, yet the original seems to have been quickly forgotten.

Tirso's play can be characterized as average Spanish tragicomedy of the Golden Age. Most of its episodes could have been invented by any professional dramatist of the epoch, or rather pulled out of the common file. A few seductions, disguises and mistaken identities, the themes of honor and revenge, a funny servant, an indignant father, a couple of pastoral episodes in the flowery rhetoric of Arcadia—this was the regular diet of the Spanish theatre-goer.

The only scenes that did distinguish *El Burlador* from other plays are those concerning the Statue. Here Tirso drew on an old Spanish ballad. This was not an unusual step to take for a Spanish playwright: ballads gave writers many of their ideas. But Tirso developed rudimentary material with unusual skill, and succeeded in adapting an ancient tale of insult to a dead man followed by the corpse's revenge to the requirements of fashionable cloak-and-dagger drama.

Tirso could have written his play without the dead man's revenge, for as the play proceeds, Don Juan is stalked by a small army of living victims. But the Statue gave him a conclusion agreeable both to the instincts of a

[1] This Introduction is based on various portions of *The Theatre of Don Juan*, edited by Oscar Mandel (Lincoln: University of Nebraska Press, 1963), in which the three plays in this collection first appeared.

vii

popular playwright and the piety of a monk in the Order of Our Lady of Ransom. For although Master Tirso might wink, Brother Gabriel would have insisted on the seriousness of the Statue. It did not descend from its pedestal to amuse the groundlings, but to preach the doctrine of timely repentance. Tirso put the best of his passion into the last act. It might have disconcerted him to know that Don Juan was to be remembered for his seductions rather than for his neglect of the sacraments—or that the Statue was to become a figure of fun in a hundred farces and puppet plays.

However Tirso's contemporaries reacted to the theological matter of the play—which is a sermon not against heresy or atheism but against indifference to the Church—modern readers appreciate the play for its sheer vitality and movement—Madariaga speaks of its "waves of energy"—and for the headlong character of Don Juan himself. The hero, without being profoundly studied, is quite the Spaniard whom Stendhal describes in the forty-seventh chapter of *De l'Amour:* "hard, abrupt, not very elegant, full of fierce pride, never concerned about anyone else." His two gods, says Pí y Margall, are "honor y placer," reputation and pleasure. He is self-reliant, forceful, impetuous, clever, eloquent, and incorrigibly stubborn. Although he is the very type of sensuality, he seems to love the jest itself as much as physical possession. The title of the play stresses the pranks rather than the sensuality. Tirso's hero owes as much to the tricksters of medieval farces, fabliaux, and *novelle* as to the Renaissance figure of the refined courtier.

The women too are drawn with a rough hand. Tirso, incapable of sentimentality, takes their little duplicities for granted. Isabela is thoroughly unscrupulous, Anna brazenly invites her cousin into her room even though her father has bestowed her on Don Juan, Arminta forgets her husband in a trice, and when Tisbea attempts suicide, it is not because her tender heart is broken, but because her reputation is lost. The type of Elvira, cheated, abandoned, but still in love, is missing altogether. Don Juan's victims know how to hit back.

El Burlador de Sevilla is still an excellent romp, in spite of its many faults. When we consider that in the post-classical versions of the story Don Juan is often saved in the end, that in his lifetime he is often pictured as looking desperately for the ideal woman, and that he is usually portrayed as fatally irresistible to every woman he meets, we are likely to feel gratitude for Tirso's tough common sense. Still, to praise *El Burlador* as a masterpiece of the human intellect is to make the mistake of ascribing the significance of the mythical hero to the vehicle which first carried him. Unlike

Hamlet, but like Faust, Don Juan was not born in a work as important as his own person.[2]

Tirso's play was soon exported to Spanish Naples and other Italian cities, where it begot a number of imitations, mostly farcical. These were the great days of the ambulant Italian players with their semi-improvised plays combining romantic intrigue, sensational "machines," and gags of every description. *El Burlador de Sevilla* had all the necessary ingredients, and by 1640 its Italian imitations were widely known. From Italy the *commedia dell'arte* troupes brought various versions into France. In 1658 a *Convitato di pietra* was performed in Paris in the very theatre used by Molière's newly-arrived company. Two French versions followed. When Molière himself took up the subject in 1665, he did not have to look into his own imagination for the basic scenes of his play.

And yet it is probably the strangest of all his plays: an anarchy of un-related scenes, false anticipations, loose ends, and tantalizingly unex-plained matters. It is a masterpiece, but one that would be laughed out of an elementary playwriting class.

The play's history is as checkered as its structure. *Dom Juan ou le Festin de Pierre* stands between two giants, *Tartuffe* (1664) and *Le Misanthrope* (1666). The three together—all onslaughts on hypocrisy—may be called the dark plays of Molière's comic career. From the moment *Tartuffe* appeared on the stage, it brought down on Molière's head libels, inter-dictions, hatreds, and plots against which he fought for five years to partial victory. *Dom Juan* in particular shows his preoccupation with the charge of freethinking that was often levelled at him—not without good cause. It seems to have been composed as a hasty counterattack. As such it failed, but the very haste, the lack of finish, the nervous rawness of this work enable us to see the true grain of Molière's mind more clearly than in any of his other plays.

Dom Juan was exhibited to the public a total of fifteen times. Coming as it did nine months after *Tartuffe* had been prohibited, the new play only made more trouble for the embattled Molière. After the first performance he was forced to suppress the capital scene with the beggar (III, 2) and to tone down other passages. The pamphleteers did not relent. Whether

---

[2] The English translation presented here is based on two texts: the 1630 text already mentioned and an undated but earlier version entitled *Tan largo me lo fiáis*, which differs substantially from the 1630 version. Neither version can claim absolute validity, and authorities like Gerald E. Wade and Albert E. Sloman agree that Tirso's original work is lost.

Molière felt that his clumsy play was not worth a fight, or whether he decided he could not sustain a war on two fronts, we have no way of knowing; but he took the king's benevolent advice (and a pension with it), withdrew the play, and never saw it thereafter in print or on stage. In 1682, nine years after his death, a badly censored text appeared in France. But the Dutch printed a genuine text in 1683, though it remained unknown until its rediscovery in the nineteenth century.

The odd paradox of *Dom Juan* is that while Molière consigns his hero to hell with one hand (in tune with the tradition), he removes most of the reasons for damning him with the other. A couple of Molière's predecessors had turned Don Juan into a parricide. Molière cut this episode. He also omitted the murder of the Octavio type which his predecessors had introduced, and in fact reversed the situation, so that we see Don Juan saving the life of the character who most nearly resembles Octavio. Moreover, having eliminated the character of Anna, he could not even provide Don Juan with the basic murder, that of the girl's infuriated father. A Commander is mentioned in the play, but we do not know who he is or why Don Juan killed him. When the Statue finally appears, neither we nor Molière can say exactly why it is there.

And what was an audience to think when this noble rogue, for whom the playwright seems to be making excuses, turns out to be an arrant and vocal atheist? For this Don Juan is unforgettably the man who believes, and believes *only*, that "two plus two equals four, and four plus four equals eight," a seemingly harmless opinion which constitutes in reality the most brazen statement any writer living under Louis XIV would ever permit himself.

True, Molière's Don Juan is "un grand seigneur méchant homme," cruel to Elvira, his father, and his creditor. But no one in the play is capable of refuting his skepticism (Molière is wicked enough to make the fool Sganarelle the defender of the faith), he behaves honorably toward Elvira's brother, he has the last and significant word in the encounter with the beggar, he plainly speaks for Molière on the question of medicine, and even his hypocrisy is really an attack on the society which almost demands this vice, rather than on Don Juan himself.

It is an error to seek to unify the play. It fascinates *because* of its contradictions. The impression we finally get is that Molière would gladly have used Don Juan as the spokesman for his own subversive views if he had dared. But he knew that the king, though his friend, would not protect him beyond a given point. The play therefore remains irresolute, advancing in favor of Don Juan the father of the Encyclopedists, and then retreating again by showing him off as a villain. This leaves us with a remarkable human document, in which we catch in the raw the unresolved contradiction between individual free thought and official decency.

With Tirso de Molina, Don Juan is a duly baroque character, tragic jester in a turmoil of sinister activity; with Molière he becomes a courtly libertine whom the wits could wink at a small distance away from the throne. Lorenzo da Ponte's hero, in turn, is all eighteenth-century Venice, that is to say utterly refined and philosophically vacant.

The Signore Abbate Da Ponte, priest, poet, and rake, had met Mozart in Vienna in 1783. In 1786 he had written the libretto for *The Marriage of Figaro*. In 1787 two operas on the subject of Don Giovanni were being performed in Rome. Da Ponte suggested that Mozart compose a third. It appears that Mozart worked with him on the libretto. In his old age (which he spent in America) Da Ponte asserted that while he urged the comic vein, Mozart, whose father had just died, wished him to write an entirely serious work. The well-known emotional oscillations of the opera may be the result of this collaboration of opposite though friendly purposes. The premiere in Prague is of course one of the famous episodes in the history of music. Da Ponte was happy: "The Emperor sent for me, and overloading me with gracious felicitations, presented me with another hundred sequins." Two years later Da Ponte was to write the jewel of all librettos, *Così fan tutte*. But from then on he took a downhill slope, surviving for another forty-eight years into a different epoch and an alien culture.

Although Mozart's work is the supreme expression of the Don Juan motif, Da Ponte deserves more than the bone usually thrown to him. Out of Molière, Goldoni, Bertati, and who knows what popular farces and puppet plays, he created a fresh and original comedy in the rococo manner, quite as pleasant as many a pleasant comedy out of Goldoni's workshop. On the philosophical or moral side, Da Ponte will not give anyone a headache. But his play shows the hand of a refined artist. We owe to him the heroic character of Anna, as well as the immortal " one thousand and three," the idea for which he probably took from one of the *Anacreontea*. The personages of the play are feather-light but alive. If the rhetoric of Anna, Elvira, and Ottavio is fustian, the modern director will turn this to his advantage and allow the three to strut and to orate to their hearts' content.

The action alternates delicately between the comic and the pathetic. Don Juan himself is as unlucky as a novice—he reports only one middling success—and yet we are convinced that he is cock of the walk. He seems incapable of premeditated murder, for he is far too fond of good wines, pretty girls, and fine dinners to be really brutal. Reading the text alone, nothing prepares us for Mozart's shattering transformation of the routine "Speak, speak! I am listening to you" that Don Giovanni addresses to the Statue, and all that follows. What had gone in as powdered wig comes out as the locks of the Medusa. Da Ponte himself was not built on heroic or tragic lines. What we remember him for is the irresistible

> Vivan le femmine!
> Viva il buon vino!
> Sostegno e gloria
> D'umanità!

But Mozart, sprightly as well as sublime, knew how to be bewitched by such words.

OSCAR MANDEL

California Institute of Technology

FOR FURTHER READING

The three basic works in English are, in chronological order, John Austen, *The Story of Don Juan* (London: Martin Secker, 1939); Leo Weinstein, *The Metamorphoses of Don Juan* (Stanford: Stanford University Press, 1959); and Oscar Mandel, *The Theatre of Don Juan: A Collection of Plays and Views, 1660–1963* (Lincoln: University of Nebraska Press, 1963).

TIRSO DE MOLINA

The Playboy of Seville

or

Supper with a Statue

(1616?)

Translated by Adrienne Schizzano Mandel
and Oscar Mandel

TRANSLATORS' NOTE

El Burlador, like most Spanish and English plays of its epoch, moves its actors rapidly from place to place. The shifts from Naples to Tarragona, from Tarragona to Seville, from Seville to Dos Hermanas, as well as the shifts within Seville—a square, a street, another street, the palace, a church—are all made without interruption in the playing. The stage of city theatres was usually bare (a simple prop or two occasionally appeared), there was no curtain to separate it from the audience, and actors marked a change of scene by vanishing through one door and reappearing through another, or by informing the audience of their whereabouts in so many words. As in the English theatre, an inner room at the back of the stage, curtained off from the main platform, could be used for interior scenes. (It is there, no doubt, that the Statue of the Commander was revealed.) An upstairs gallery over the inner room was used for scenes requiring altitude. The female parts, incidentally, were performed by actresses, and not, as in England, by boy actors. For a full account, see Hugo A. Rennert, *The Spanish Stage in the Time of Lope de Vega* (New York: Hispanic Society of America, 1909).

TEXTS

¿Tan largo me lo fiáis? in *Comedias de Tirso de Molina*, vol. II. Edited by Emilio Cotarelo y Mori. Madrid: Bailly-Baillere, 1907. *El Burlador de Sevilla y Convidado de piedra* in *Tirso de Molina: Obras*, vol. I. Edited by Américo Castro. Clásicos Castellanos. Madrid: Espasa-Calpe, 1932.

Persons in the Play

The King of Castile
The King of Naples
Don Diego Tenorio
Don Juan Tenorio, *his son*
Don Pedro Tenorio, *brother of Don Diego; Spanish Ambassador at the court of Naples*
Duke Octavio
Duchess Isabela
Marquis de la Mota
Don Gonzalo de Ulloa, *Commander of the Order of Calatrava*
Doña Ana, *his daughter*
Tisbea, *a fishergirl*
Anfriso, *her admirer*

Tirseo
Alfredo
Salucis
Coridon

} *fishermen*

Belisa, *a rustic maiden*
Arminta, *a shepherdess*
Batricio, *her betrothed*
Gaceno, *her father*
Catalinón, *servant to Don Juan*
Ripio, *servant of Duke Octavio*
Fabio, *companion to Duchess Isabela*
A Woman

Fishermaids, fishermen, shepherds and shepherdesses, servants, musicians, guards of the palace, courtiers

Synopsis of Scenes

Act I

1. A hall in the palace of the King of Naples.
2. Duke Octavio's palace, Naples.
3. A beach near Tarragona.
4. A room in the Alcázar, the palace of the King of Castile, Seville.
5. Near the cottage of Tisbea, Tarragona.

Act II

1. A room in the Alcázar, Seville.
2. The city of Seville.
3. Near the village of Dos Hermanas.

Act III

1. Gaceno's house, Dos Hermanas.
2. Near Tarragona.
3. Inside a church, Seville.
4. An inn, Seville.
5. A room in the Alcázar.
6. The Fortress of Triana.
7. Before the church.
8. A room in the Alcázar.

ACT I

Scene 1

Night. A hall in the palace of the King of Naples. Enter DON JUAN TENORIO *and the* DUCHESS ISABELA. *His face is hidden.*

ISABELA: Leave quietly, Duke Octavio.

DON JUAN: I'll be light as a feather.

ISABELA: Still—I'm afraid you'll be heard. You know it's a crime to enter the palace at night.

DON JUAN [*in the act of leaving*]: At another time, Duchess, I will express my gratitude for your favors.

ISABELA: You've given me your hand in marriage.

DON JUAN: The gainer is myself.

ISABELA: I ventured my honor because of your pledge to be my husband.

DON JUAN: I am your husband, and I give you my hand again.

ISABELA: Wait! Here is a light. I want to see my good fortune. Oh God!

DON JUAN: Put out that light!

ISABELA: I'm ruined. Who are you?

DON JUAN: A man who has enjoyed you.

ISABELA: You're not the Duke?

DON JUAN: No.

ISABELA: Who are you? Speak!

DON JUAN: A man.

ISABELA: Your name?

DON JUAN: I have no name.

ISABELA: A trickster has seduced me. Help! Help!

DON JUAN: Wait.

ISABELA: Take your hand away! Villain!

DON JUAN: Don't scream.

ISABELA: Help! Guards! Guards!

[*Enter* KING OF NAPLES.]

KING OF NAPLES: What is it?

ISABELA: The King! Everything is lost!

KING OF NAPLES: Who is there?

DON JUAN: Can't you see? A man and a woman.

[handwritten note: starts to worry about her honor]

5

KING OF NAPLES [*Aside.*]: This calls for caution. I'll try to smooth things over.

[*Enter* DON PEDRO, *the Spanish Ambassador, and* SOLDIERS.]

DON PEDRO: My lord, I heard voices. What is the matter?

KING OF NAPLES: Have these two arrested and punished.

DON PEDRO: Who are they?

KING OF NAPLES: It's better for me not to know. Don't arouse me. I'm trying to control myself, and I know their guilt as it is. Don Pedro Tenorio, I charge you to make the arrest. Find out who these two are, and see to everything else.

[*Exit* KING OF NAPLES.]

DON PEDRO: Give yourself up, sir.

DON JUAN: If anybody touches me, I'll kill him.

DON PEDRO [*to soldiers*]: Kill him!

DON JUAN: You're giving them poor advice. Tell them to put up their swords. If I have to die, I'll take all of you along for consolation. I warn you!

SOLDIER: Die, villain!

DON JUAN: Fool! I'm a gentleman.

DON PEDRO: This is too much!

DON JUAN: Stop! Leave me with the Spanish Ambassador. I'll surrender to him alone.

DON PEDRO: Now you're speaking sensibly. Leave, all of you, and take this woman along.

ISABELA [*Aside.*]: How can one man be so vicious! I have lost my honor and lost Octavio.

[*Exeunt* ISABELA *and soldiers.*]

DON PEDRO: Show your courage and strength now that we're alone.

DON JUAN: I have strength, Uncle, but I never used it against you.

DON PEDRO: Who are you?

DON JUAN: Don Juan.

DON PEDRO: Don Juan?

DON JUAN: Yes, my lord.

DON PEDRO: And you say it just like that?

DON JUAN: End my life and with it all my misery.

DON PEDRO: Traitor. A man without honor can't be my nephew. You with a woman in the King's palace? And you dare outrage my name with this crime?

DON JUAN: Uncle, I don't want you to delay—arrest me if you must. But remember, it was love that drove me to this. A man who loves is blind. I am young. You were young once.

DON PEDRO: Who is the lady?

DON JUAN: The lady is—

DON PEDRO: Who? Speak!

DON JUAN: Isabela.

DON PEDRO: The Queen's lady-in-waiting?

DON JUAN: I duped her by pretending to be Duke Octavio.

DON PEDRO: Worse! Your father sent you from Castile to Naples for committing the same crime against a noblewoman there. Italy gave you asylum, but still you continue your scandalous life, sparing neither single nor married women. And now, with a duchess, in the palace itself! I would have killed you on the spot. But you're the blood of my blood, and I must let you go. Where to now?

DON JUAN: Here is a balcony.

DON PEDRO: Climb over it and down.

DON JUAN: It's high but I'll use my cape.

DON PEDRO: Just don't startle the King again. I'll tell him you escaped through a window.

DON JUAN: It's almost day.

DON PEDRO: The only thing you can do is leave Naples and go back to Spain. If I can convince the King with my story, I'll try to marry you to Isabela and force you to wipe off this blot.

DON JUAN: Sir, you honor me.

DON PEDRO: You'll have letters from me about this sad affair.

DON JUAN [*Aside.*]: Not so sad for me.

DON PEDRO: Go now. But don't forget that punishment, death, and Hell await people like you.

DON JUAN: Plenty of time for that.

DON PEDRO: Still presumptuous. Come, over the balcony.

DON JUAN [*Aside.*]: I'm off for Spain—quite satisfied with myself.

[*Exeunt* DON JUAN TENORIO *and* DON PEDRO TENORIO. *Enter* KING OF NAPLES.]

KING OF NAPLES: Men envy the king's crown but they don't know its price. They know only how to complain about having to live under its law. But I envy simple cattle herders and tillers of the land. They live by their sweat but they don't suffer injustice nor do they rule nations. For let a king have a thousand eyes and still he must be all ears, must listen to complaints and avenge the wrongs of the country.

[*Enter* DON PEDRO TENORIO.]

DON PEDRO: My lord, while I was carrying out your orders, the man—

KING OF NAPLES: Died?

DON PEDRO: Escaped.

KING OF NAPLES: What?

DON PEDRO: Who would believe it? The guards and I attacked him. Like a desperate man, judging us weak, he began to strike back ferociously. I cried, "Kill him!" He tied his cape to the railing of the balcony and fell like Lucifer. I ran and saw him in the moonlight writhing like a snake on the ground. I cried for help, but by the time I had gone to the door he had vanished. I thought it best to pursue no further in order to prevent a scandal.

KING OF NAPLES: You're a wise man, Ambassador. But I am very sorry the man wasn't killed. Do you know who the lady is?

DON PEDRO: My lord, it is the Duchess Isabela.

KING OF NAPLES: What did you say?

DON PEDRO: What you heard.

KING OF NAPLES: Then the offence is more serious and the man of more importance. Send for her.

[Enter ISABELA.]

ISABELA [Aside.]: How can I look at the King?

KING OF NAPLES [Aside.]: I am ashamed to see her.

ISABELA [Aside.]: Love, give me courage.

KING OF NAPLES: Duchess!

ISABELA: My lord, I confess. Let my punishment be my shame in your presence. Yes, I violated your palace. After Duke Octavio had given me his hand in marriage, he gained admission to the palace, to my soul, and to my dearest possession. My chastity, my honesty are lost.

KING OF NAPLES: You're saying it was Duke Octavio?

ISABELA: Yes, my lord.

KING OF NAPLES: What good are guards, servants, walls, and fortifications against Love, which is a child and yet breaks through them all! Don Pedro, arrest the Duke—and this woman too.

ISABELA: My lord, turn your face to me.

KING OF NAPLES: You offended me when my back was turned. Justice demands that now I turn mine to you.

[Exit KING OF NAPLES.]

DON PEDRO: The King is justly offended with my lady.

ISABELA [Aside.]: The offence will be slight if Duke Octavio makes amends.

DON PEDRO: Come, my lady. [Aside.] If I can, I'll have the innocent Duke acquitted—and I'll see my nephew married to Isabela.

[Exeunt DON PEDRO and ISABELA.]

Scene 2

Duke Octavio's palace in Naples. Morning. Enter DUKE OCTAVIO *and* RIPIO.

RIPIO: Up so early, sir!

OCTAVIO: To a man in love, rest is impossible. Have you seen a wretch struggling among the waves until the foaming sea engulfs him? My bed is that sea. I drown under the cold sky, I suffer at night, and only daylight rescues me from my torment.

RIPIO: Forgive me. But I find your love impertinent.

OCTAVIO: You're a fool.

RIPIO: I think it's impertinent to love as you do. May I go on?

OCTAVIO: All right—continue.

RIPIO: Does Isabela love you?

OCTAVIO: How can you doubt it?

RIPIO: Just an academic question. You love her too?

OCTAVIO: I do!

RIPIO: Well, wouldn't I be a fool to lose my senses for a woman who loves me and whom I love in return? Now if she did not love you, it would be reasonable to persist, adore her and shower her with gifts and wait patiently for her surrender. But if you love each other equally, what prevents you two from marrying?

OCTAVIO: Fool! You expect me to marry like a lackey or a washerwoman?

RIPIO: What's wrong with a washerwoman? She scrubs and gossips and jokes as she spreads her wash out to dry. As for giving—she is very generous. And if Isabela doesn't feel like giving, see if she will take. [*Enter* SECOND SERVANT.]

SECOND SERVANT: The Spanish Ambassador has just arrived accompanied by the King's guard. He is asking with rough words to speak to you, as though he had come to arrest you.

OCTAVIO: Arrest me? For what? I have nothing to fear. Show him in. [*Enter* DON PEDRO *and others.*]

DON PEDRO: Only an innocent man can sleep so late.

OCTAVIO: Your visit honors me, Your Excellency. My crime is not to have met a gentleman like you at the door.

DON PEDRO: I was forced to come.

OCTAVIO: I know that only force would prevail upon a man of your rank to enter this house. But humble as it is, I place it at your disposal.

DON PEDRO: After kissing your hand, my lord, I should like to speak with you alone about a certain affair.

OCTAVIO [to Servants]: Leave us alone.

RIPIO: Yes, sir.

OCTAVIO: Clear out the room.

SECOND SERVANT [to Ripio]: This means prison.

RIPIO [to Second Servant]: I think you're right.

SECOND SERVANT: Envy's at the bottom of this.

[Exeunt RIPIO and SECOND SERVANT.]

OCTAVIO: We're alone.

DON PEDRO: Excellency, look at this paper.

OCTAVIO [reads]: "Arrest Duke Octavio, and if he resists, let him die. The King." Arrest! What have I done?

DON PEDRO: You know better than I. Last night there was a scandalous disturbance at the palace, offensive to the King and to the people. As the shadows of the night folded their tents and, stumbling against each other, fled before the coming of dawn, I was discussing with His Majesty certain problems of state (great matters are enemies of the sun). Suddenly we heard a woman's cries echo through the dark halls: "Help, help!" The King rushed out with a light—bold as always—and in the great hall he saw the cause of the uproar. I joined him with the Captain of the Guards and other gentlemen. "Arrest this man and this woman," said the King, and left us. The man blew out the light before we could recognize him. We threw ourselves on him, but he escaped from us like a Libyan tiger and fled over a balcony. We decided not to pursue him for fear of alarming the court. We reported to the King. The lady, whose name is Isabela—I say it to confound you—was brought into the presence of the King and confessed with tears and sobs that Duke Octavio had enjoyed her as her husband. The King ordered her arrest and yours. Listen to me. I am your friend: run away or hide in a safe place.

OCTAVIO: Either you're jesting or I'm dreaming. A man with Isabela in the Palace? I'll go mad. Before I believe that Isabela deceived me, salamanders will inhabit the lowest depths of the stormy seas and fish will seek fire instead of water. I am ashamed to listen to you. A man with Isabela in the Palace? I have gone mad.

DON PEDRO: As there are birds in the wind; fish in the sea; four elements for all creatures to share, and saints in heaven; as there is loyalty in a good friend, deceit in the enemy, darkness at night, light in the day—so what I have told you is true.

OCTAVIO: Enough! Tell me no evil against Isabela. And yet—if her love was a lie, you are right to speak out. Speak, speak! Your tongue draws my blood, but this is a gentle death, a blessing for my grief. With another man and not with me? But why wait?—Let me kill my enemy. What am I saying? This is madness. But what consolation is sanity to me? My friend, a man with Isabela in the palace? I have gone mad. Nothing astonishes me. The most faithful of women is, after all, only a woman. The affront is clear and I want to know no more.

DON PEDRO: You seem both prudent and wise. Choose the best way out.

OCTAVIO: I'll leave.

DON PEDRO: But quickly, Duke Octavio.

OCTAVIO: I'll sail for Spain to end all my troubles.

DON PEDRO: I suggest the door of the garden.

OCTAVIO: Oh weathervane! A feeble reed that bends before the softest wind! Come, I'm pouring oil on my fire. Away from this nest of deceit to another land. Farewell, my country! A man with Isabela? I have gone mad!

Scene 3

A beach near Tarragona. A young woman, TISBEA, *enters with a fishing pole.*

TISBEA: Of all the girls whose rosy feet the waves kiss on these shores, I alone am not ruled by love. I sail in my little boat with my companions. I like to catch the little fish lashed by the waves. I wander free from the prisons which love fills with fools. My only pleasure is to give the fish my baited line. Others suffer and mourn, but I spend my youth without a care. I let the silly fish leap into my net, and I alone do not fall into the snares of love. Meantime Anfriso is my slave, a fisherman, the most generous and gentle man in the land. All the women would die for him; I instead kill him with disdain. This is the game of love: to love those who hate you, and to despise those who adore you. In the cold night Anfriso keeps watch about my hut, and every morning, even in cold weather, my threshhold is adorned with fresh boughs which he has cut from the elms. He sere-

nades me sweetly with flute or guitar. But nothing impresses me because I live beyond the reach of love. But all this silly talk is taking me away from my favorite pastime and my one desire—to cast my line to the wind and waves. Look! A boat foundering in the sea! And two men leaping off! It struck the reef and now it's sinking!
[*Voice off stage: "Help, I'm drowning!"*]

A man is carrying the one who screamed. He is carrying his friend on his back and bravely saving him as Aeneas saved Anchises. But there's no one on the beach to help. Anfriso, Tirseo, Alfredo, help! I see some fishermen looking at me—I hope they hear me. What a miracle! They've touched shore! And now the man who was swimming is out of breath and the one who cried out has gained strength.
[*Enter* CATALINÓN, *carrying* DON JUAN *in his arms. Both are wet.*]

CATALINÓN: Ugh! So much salt in that sea! Near the beach a man can swim and save himself, but farther out it's deathly dangerous. How could God put together so much water and not add a little wine? And if he had to fill the sea with water, why all that salt? That's too much for somebody like me who doesn't even fish. If fresh water is bad for a man's health, imagine what all that salt will do to me! I really need a bit of wine now.

If I survive all the water I drank today, I make a vow to abstain from it forever; I'll even refrain from looking at the holy water. Master, you're cold and stiff! Are you dead? The sea is responsible but they'll naturally blame me for it. Cursed be the man who first sowed pine trees in the sea and the man who first sailed in the fragility of wood. And curses on Jason and Tiphys! He's dead. Unbelievable! Catalinón, Catalinón, where can you go now?

TISBEA: What's the matter, my good man?

CATALINÓN: Ah, fishermaid, much evil and little good. My master died trying to save me. Look for yourself. What shall I do?

TISBEA: You're wrong. He's still breathing.

CATALINÓN: Where? Here?

TISBEA: Naturally; where else?

CATALINÓN: He might be breathing out in another place.

TISBEA: Fool.

CATALINÓN: I want to kiss your snowy hands.

TISBEA: Why don't you call the fishermen in that hut over there?

CATALINÓN: Will they come if I call?

TISBEA: Of course. Who is this gentleman?

CATALINÓN: He is the son of the King's Chamberlain. He's going to make me count as soon as we get to Seville—if the King agrees, that is.

TISBEA: What's his name?

CATALINÓN: Don Juan Tenorio.

TISBEA: Go and call my people.

CATALINÓN: Right away.

[*Exit* CATALINÓN. TISBEA *places* DON JUAN's *head in her lap.*]

TISBEA: Wake up, handsomest of all men, and be yourself again.

DON JUAN: Where am I?

TISBEA: In the arms of a woman.

DON JUAN: If the sea gives me death, you give me life. But the sea really saved me only to be killed by you. Oh the sea tosses me from one torment to the other, for I no sooner pulled myself from the water than I met its siren—yourself. Why fill my ears with wax, since you kill me with your eyes? I was dying in the sea, but from today I shall die of love.

TISBEA: You have abundant breath for a man who almost drowned. You suffered much, but who knows what suffering you are preparing for me? Perhaps you're my Trojan horse, come out of the sea. I found you at my feet all water, and now you are all fire. If you burn when you are so wet, what will you do when you're dry again? You promise a scorching flame; I hope to God you're not lying.

DON JUAN: Dear girl, God should have drowned me before I could be charred by you. Perhaps love was wise to drench me before I felt your scalding touch. But your fire is such that even in water I burn.

TISBEA: So cold and yet burning?

DON JUAN: So much fire is in you.

TISBEA: How well you talk!

DON JUAN: How well you understand!

TISBEA: I hope to God you're not lying.

[*Enter four fishermen*—ANFRISO, TIRSEO, ALFREDO, *and* SALUCIO—*and* CATALINÓN.]

CATALINÓN: They've come.

TISBEA: Your master is alive.

DON JUAN: Your presence has given me the life I lost.

ANFRISO: What do you want, Tisbea? You have only to speak. Those who worship you are ready to satisfy your least desire: We are ready to furrow the earth, plow the sea, tread the fire, and arrest the wind.

TISBEA [*Aside.*]: Only yesterday these tender words sounded ridiculous to me, but today I understand that they may be true. [*Aloud.*]

Friends, I was fishing here when I saw a ship sink and these two men swim clear. I called for help but no one heard me. One of them lay lifeless on the sand. It was this gentleman whom his servant had carried out of the water. I was distressed and called for your help.

TIRSEO: We are all at your command.

TISBEA: Take them to my cottage. There we'll dry their clothes and look after them. Our kindness will please my father.

CATALINÓN [to Don Juan]: She is a marvelous woman.

DON JUAN [to Catalinón]: Listen to me.

CATALINÓN: Yes.

DON JUAN: If she asks my name, tell her you don't know me.

CATALINÓN: Are you trying to tell me what to do?

DON JUAN: I'm dying with love for her. I must enjoy her tonight.

CATALINÓN: How?

DON JUAN: Just follow me and listen. . . . [DON JUAN draws CATALINÓN aside.]

ALFREDO: Salucio, the dancing must begin within the hour.

SALUCIO: Tonight we'll dance and sing till we drop.

[Exeunt ANFRISO and other fishermen.]

DON JUAN: I'm dying.

TISBEA: But you're walking.

DON JUAN: You can see how painful it is.

TISBEA: How well you talk!

DON JUAN: How well you understand!

TISBEA: I hope to God you're not lying.

[Exeunt.]

Scene 4

A room in the Alcázar, the palace of the King of Castile, Seville. The KING OF CASTILE *enters with* DON GONZALO DE ULLOA.

KING OF CASTILE: Was your embassy successful, Don Gonzalo?

DON GONZALO: In Lisbon I found your cousin preparing thirty vessels to leave for Goa. He received me well indeed.

KING OF CASTILE: He fears the sword in the brave hand of an Ulloa. Your strength has threatened the Moor many times. Did you like Lisbon?

DON GONZALO: It's the eighth marvel of the world. Indeed, sir, it deserves to be your capital.

KING OF CASTILE: Is it larger than Seville?

DON GONZALO: No city can equal Seville.

KING OF CASTILE: Don Gonzalo, do you have children?

DON GONZALO: One daughter, my lord, whose beauty comforts my old age and encourages my efforts.

KING OF CASTILE: I intend to marry her well.

DON GONZALO: Who can possibly deserve her?

KING OF CASTILE: I know of a young gentleman in Italy of noble blood and reputation. He is the son of Don Diego, my Chamberlain, the brother of the famous Don Pedro, who represents me so well at the Neapolitan court. Your son-in-law shall be Count of Lebrija, a city his father subdued for me. I know your daughter deserves even better, but now your mind can be at ease. When we are old, peace of mind has the power to slow the galloping horse of time.

DON GONZALO: You honor me too much, my lord.

KING OF CASTILE: Go and let the good news be known.

DON GONZALO: May your life never touch the gates of oblivion.

KING OF CASTILE: Notable merit deserves an equal reward.

DON GONZALO: All Seville will know my happiness.

KING OF CASTILE: Return to me later.

DON GONZALO: Enjoy your immortal Kingdom.

[*Exeunt* KING OF CASTILE *and* DON GONZALO *in different directions.*]

Scene 5

Near the cottage of Tisbea, Tarragona. DON JUAN *enters with* CATALINÓN.

DON JUAN: Saddle the two mares while the fishermen are having their feast. When I'm in trouble I rely on flying hooves.

CATALINÓN: You've decided to seduce Tisbea?

DON JUAN: You don't think I've reformed?

CATALINÓN: I know you're the scourge of women.

DON JUAN: She's a lovely girl and I'll die without her.

CATALINÓN: You're the perfect guest.

DON JUAN: Fool! I'm as good a guest as Aeneas was to the Queen of Carthage.

CATALINÓN: You and the others like you who cheat and seduce women will pay for your pleasure with your lives.

DON JUAN: Plenty of time for that.

CATALINÓN: Here comes the lamb.

DON JUAN: Go quickly and saddle the mares.

CATALINÓN: Poor girl! You're about to be repaid for your generosity.
 [*Exit* CATALINÓN. *Enter* TISBEA.]

TISBEA: I can't stay away from you.

DON JUAN: If only I could believe your words.

TISBEA: Why not?

DON JUAN: Because if you loved me, you would be kind to me.

TISBEA: I'm yours.

DON JUAN: But if that's so—why wait? Why doubt? Why hesitate?

TISBEA: Because I think that my love for you is a punishment for my indifference of old.

DON JUAN: So is mine. For I have loved none other than you. But now I give you my word, and the hand of a husband.

TISBEA: You're a nobleman.

DON JUAN: Don't speak of such things, Tisbea. I am in your house, and I had rather be a humble fisherman here, enjoying the favors of your beautiful person, than possess all the treasures of the world.

TISBEA: I would like to believe you, but you men are all deception.

DON JUAN: Look into my eyes. Come into my arms. Kiss me, and give me your soul in that kiss.

TISBEA: I surrender to you. You are now my husband.

DON JUAN: By your beautiful and fatal eyes! I swear!

TISBEA: Remember, my love, there is hell and death.

DON JUAN [*Aside.*]: Plenty of time for that! [*Aloud.*] While I live, I am your slave.

TISBEA: Take my hand.

DON JUAN: And here is mine to set your mind at rest.

TISBEA: Our wedding bed is prepared in my cottage. Wait for me among the reeds till the time comes.

DON JUAN: And how do I enter?

TISBEA: I'll show you the way.

DON JUAN [*Aside.*]: She is blind—but satisfied.

TISBEA: May my love bind yours. If not, may God punish you.

DON JUAN [*Aside.*]: Plenty of time for that.
 [*Exeunt* DON JUAN *and* TISBEA. *Enter* CORIDON, ANFRISO, BELISA *and musicians.*]

CORIDON: Call Tisbea and the others so the guests can enjoy our performance.

ANFRISO: She must be very busy with them. They're lucky men!

CORIDON: Everybody is envious of Tisbea. Here's her house.

BELISA: This spot is better for dancing. Let's call her and the others from here: Tisbea, Lucinda, Antandra.

ALL [*singing*]: A girl went out to sea,
                She cast her net so wide
                She found, instead of fish,
                My dying soul inside.

[*Enter* TISBEA.]

TISBEA: Fire! Fire! And madness! I'm burning! My hut is burning! Sound the alarm my friends, for my soul is on fire. My own house, an instrument of my dishonor! Fire! Burning stars have kindled my tresses and winds have fanned the flames. I laughed at other girls for falling in love and now love is laughing at me. A man deceived me with a promise of marriage and violated my honesty and my bed. He enjoyed me, and I even supplied the mares for his escape to cap his joke and my disgrace. He came like a cloud from the sea to drown me. But I believed his words—and I deserve nothing better. Friends, follow him. No, I'll ask vengeance from the King. I'll go to him myself. Fire! Fire! Water! Water! Have mercy, love, my heart is in flames!

[*Exit* TISBEA.]

CORIDON: Follow her; she is so desperate she might fling herself into the sea.

BELISA: Her pride ruined her.

ANFRISO: To this her blind confidence brought her. She's running to the sea! Tisbea, wait! Listen!

BELISA: She is coming back. Hold her, don't let her run away. Hold her tight.

[*Enter* TISBEA.]

TISBEA: Fire! Fire! Have mercy, love, my heart is in flames!

[*Exeunt.*]

ACT II

Scene 1

A room in the Alcázar, Seville. Enter KING OF CASTILE *and* DON DIEGO TENORIO.

KING OF CASTILE: What are you saying?

DON DIEGO: It's true, my lord. My brother, your Ambassador, wrote it in this letter. They found my son in the King's palace with a beautiful lady. She, however, accused Duke Octavio of the crime.

KING OF CASTILE: Who is she? A lady of rank?

DON DIEGO: Duchess Isabela.

KING OF CASTILE: Isabela? The audacity! And where is your son now?

DON DIEGO: I don't want to conceal the truth from Your Majesty. He arrived in Seville last night with a servant.

KING OF CASTILE: Tenorio, you know my great esteem for you. I will send a letter immediately to the King of Naples, marry the young scamp to Isabela, and pacify the innocent Duke Octavio. But I want Don Juan banished from here at once.

DON DIEGO: Where to, my lord?

KING OF CASTILE: He must leave Seville for Lebrija tonight. I am making the sentence light only out of consideration for your merits, Don Diego. But what shall we tell Gonzalo de Ulloa? I promised your son to his daughter. How can we solve that problem?

DON DIEGO: My lord, I am ready to do whatever is called for. Don Gonzalo's high distinction—

KING OF CASTILE: I see one way of appeasing his anger: I'll make him majordomo of the palace.

[*Enter a Servant.*]

SERVANT: A gentleman is here from abroad. My lord, he says he is the Duke Octavio.

KING OF CASTILE: Duke Octavio?

SERVANT: Yes, my lord.

KING OF CASTILE: I wonder if he discovered your son's impudent trick. If so, no doubt he'll ask permission to challenge him.

DON DIEGO: My life is in your hands, Your Highness, for my real life is that of my disobedient son. Young as he is, he is already strong and courageous. Indeed, his friends call him the Hector of Seville because of his many heroic actions. Your Highness, reason with Octavio; prevent a duel.

KING OF CASTILE: Enough, Tenorio. A father's honor—

[*To Servant*] Show the Duke in.

DON DIEGO: Allow me to kiss your feet. How can I repay your favors?

[*Enter* OCTAVIO *in traveling clothes.*]

OCTAVIO: My lord, I come before you as a wretched exile and wanderer. Let me embrace your feet. Your presence mends all the miseries of my journey.

KING OF CASTILE: Duke Octavio. . . .

OCTAVIO: I have fled the rank frivolity of a woman and the unintentional injustice of a king; though I should not say so, for the law shines clear in the mirror of kings. A woman lightly deceived the King, accusing me of seduction in the palace. But I trust in time to disabuse him and to make my innocence clear.

KING OF CASTILE: Duke, I know you are innocent. I will ask the King of Naples to restore your possessions and to make amends for the losses you are suffering during your absence. Moreover, I will marry you in Seville if you wish, and if the King of Naples agrees. Though Isabela may seem an angel of beauty, she is ugly beside the wife I shall be giving you. She is the daughter of Don Gonzalo de Ulloa, Grand Commander of Calatrava, the terror of the Moors. Her virtue, which is second only to her beauty, would be a sufficient dowry in itself. And this sun among the stars of Castile shall be your wife.

OCTAVIO: My lord, you have made my journey my happiness. Your wish is my command.

KING OF CASTILE [to Don Diego]: Lodge the Duke comfortably.

OCTAVIO: The man who trusts in you, my lord, is well rewarded. Though you are Alfonso the Eleventh, you are truly the first Alfonso. [Exeunt all.]

Scene 2

The City of Seville. DUKE OCTAVIO *and his servant* RIPIO *enter from different sides.*

RIPIO: Well, what happened?

OCTAVIO: I am too happy to speak.

RIPIO: Any success?

OCTAVIO: Much gained and little lost. His Highness received me with the most loving condescension. His favors have ended my troubles. He asks me to remain in Seville, and I am madly anxious to please him.

RIPIO: And did he find you a wife?

OCTAVIO: Yes, my friend; a native of Seville. You are surprised, but Seville produces not only the strongest and liveliest men, but also the most graceful women. In short, you see me perfectly consoled.

RIPIO: I take it Isabela no longer keeps you awake.

OCTAVIO: Right.

[Enter DON JUAN and CATALINÓN.]

CATALINÓN: Wait. The Duke. Isabela's Sagittarius—or rather her Capricorn.*

DON JUAN: Don't give us away.

CATALINÓN [*Aside*.]: He'll flatter him after stabbing him in the back.

DON JUAN [*to Octavio*]: Octavio! Forgive me for not taking leave of you. I was called away from Naples suddenly on business of the King.

OCTAVIO: And you find me here, my friend, for the same reason.

DON JUAN: Who would have thought we'd meet again in Seville? And that you'd leave the lovely coast of Naples?

OCTAVIO: Naples is beautiful, but Seville is a fair match for it.

DON JUAN: When did you arrive?

OCTAVIO: Yesterday.

DON JUAN: Splendid! I want you to savor all the beauties of Seville. Twelve gates, ramparts with magnificent views over the countryside, a river—the Guadalquivir—next to which your Tiber is a teardrop— and alongside the river charming sirens no one stops his ears against. One look at our Alcázar would have made the Trojans forget Troy and the Babylonians their hanging gardens. The Hall of the Kings is so rich you'd think Jupiter held court there in his shower of gold. Its fifty-four pillars grunt under the weight. Did I say pillars? I should have said towers, and even towers are like twigs compared to them. As for the cathedral, it is so huge that only a lynx can see from one portal to another. Every day two hundred masses are sung at its two famous altars. Where is Heaven served more majestically? Neither in Rome nor in Toledo, if Toledo will forgive my saying so. Its tower is surmounted by a bronze weathervane representing Faith. We call it La Giralda—that is to say, "The Fickle Woman." During Holy Week you will see the most astounding processions—sixty of them—pouring rubies over God like floods of blood. Seville also has more than a hundred convents, two of them so large they are cities in themselves, and twelve hospitals for the poor. A genuine Ribera hangs in one of them.

In the streets the traders scramble and compete, major guilds, minor guilds—a perpetual come-and-go. Ships that have seen the boundary of dawn and the kingdom of night unload their pearls, coral, amethysts, embroideries, brocades, the finest fabrics—and everything the sun, the earth, and the sea engender for man to enjoy and squander. Besides this, the women are handsome, spirited, and

*Octavio, who was once Isabela's protector (in the Zodiac, Sagittarius is the Archer), has become a cuckold (Capricorn is the Goat). [*Translator's note.*]

proud—sorceresses when they talk, but constant, chaste, and firm in their actions—except when they are riding in their closed carriages. Curses on Pharaoh who invented them! . . . Well, such is Seville, and believe me I have been too brief in my praises.*

OCTAVIO: If I had heard your description in Naples before I came here, I would have laughed at you. But now that I see it, I must confess I don't think any praise of Seville exaggerated. But who is the man coming this way?

DON JUAN: The Marquis de la Mota.

OCTAVIO: Well, allow me to take my leave.

DON JUAN: If you need me, my sword is at your command.

CATALINÓN [Aside.]: And he'll take your name if he needs it to seduce another woman, like the scoundrel he is.

OCTAVIO: I am obliged to you.

[Exit OCTAVIO.]

CATALINÓN [to Ripio]: If I can be of any use to you, you'll always find me ready for you.

RIPIO: Where are you staying?

CATALINÓN: At the Sign of the Sparrow—a tavernacle of wine, my friend.

[Exit RIPIO. Enter MARQUIS DE LA MOTA accompanied by his SERVANT.]

MARQUIS [to Don Juan]: I have been looking for you all day without finding you. Don Juan! You are in Seville, and here's your friend pining away in your absence.

---

*A kind of guided tour of Seville, more than 650 lines long, is condensed in this speech, which replaces Ulloa's equally long and even more extraneous description of Lisbon in *El Burlador*.

In a private communication, Professor Gerald E. Wade refers to the *Cuadros viejos* of Julio Monreal for an explanation of the passage concerning the carriages: "The Spanish thought that the carriage was invented by the Germans, and hence it was for a time looked upon as a foreign thing and a sort of Lutheran devil, a *vicio infernal* that caused men to loll at their decadent ease rather than ride on horseback as he-men should, and that caused women to lose their chastity. The *coche* was accused of being a frequent place for love-trysts, much like the automobile today. Tirso cracks in *Desde Toledo a Madrid*

> que hay hembra que una noche
> no se acostó, por solo andar en coche—

there was a woman who couldn't go to bed one night, she was too sore from lying down in a coach. The *coche* became a status symbol of great importance, and—when the owner's means permitted—was decorated in every extravagant way possible, something like a deluxe convertible with us. The traffic problem in the center of cities became acute. . . ." [*Translator's note*.]

Don Juan: By God, my friend, you do me great honor.

Catalinón [*Aside.*]: If it doesn't concern women or anything that interests him, you can trust him to act like a gentleman.

Don Juan: What's new in Seville?

Marquis: Things have changed at court.

Don Juan: And the women?

Marquis: The women too.

Don Juan: What about Inès?

Marquis: Going to Vejel.

Don Juan: Good resort for a great lady like her.

Marquis: The years are driving her there.

Don Juan: To die. And her sister?

Marquis: She's a sorry sight: her head and brows completely bald. But she still thinks everybody admires her, and affects to mistake even an insult for a compliment.

Don Juan: And Theodora?

Marquis: This summer she cured herself of the French disease by sweating it out. And now she is so affectionate that day before yesterday she pulled a tooth of mine—whispering gentle words all the time.

Don Juan: And Julia of Candle Street?

Marquis: Fights on, armed with her cosmetic box.

Don Juan: Still thinks of herself as caviar?

Marquis: No; just plain cod by now.

Don Juan: And the Catarranas district: still crowded?

Marquis: Yes. With harpies.

Don Juan: Are those two sisters still alive?

Marquis: Yes, also that monkey of Tolù and their mother Celestina, who teaches them all her tricks.

Don Juan: The old witch! What about the older daughter?

Marquis: Blanca? Penniless. But she found a saint for whom she can fast.

Don Juan: Vigils and all?

Marquis: Oh, she's a holy woman now.

Don Juan: And the other?

Marquis: More practical; she doesn't reject any rubbish.

Don Juan: Like a good builder. Tell me, Marquis, have you played any tricks lately?

Marquis: Last night Esquivel and I made terrors of ourselves. For tonight we've got two little adventures planned.

Don Juan: I'll come along. However, I also want to visit a little nest where I left a few eggs hatching for us. But what about your love affairs?

MARQUIS: I've forgotten all about them. I have higher cares these days.

DON JUAN: How so?

MARQUIS: I desire the impossible.

DON JUAN: Ah. She's not interested.

MARQUIS: That's not it. She loves me.

DON JUAN: Who is she?

MARQUIS: My cousin Doña Ana, who arrived recently in Seville.

DON JUAN: From where?

MARQUIS: Lisbon. Her father is the Ambassador.

DON JUAN: Is she beautiful?

MARQUIS: Extremely. Nature excelled itself in creating Doña Ana.

DON JUAN: That beautiful! By God, I must see her.

MARQUIS: You will see the greatest beauty under the sun.

DON JUAN: Marry her, if she is so beautiful.

MARQUIS: The King has given her away already, nobody knows to whom.

DON JUAN: Does she love you?

MARQUIS: She writes to me. . . .

CATALINÓN [*Aside.*]: Say no more—the greatest scoundrel of Spain is about to trick you.

DON JUAN: Why be miserable if you are completely satisfied with her? Bring her out, woo her, write to her, seduce her, and the consequences be damned!

MARQUIS: I am waiting to hear her final resolution now.

DON JUAN: Don't waste more time—find out—I'll look for you here later.

MARQUIS: Good-bye then.

CATALINÓN [*to the Marquis' servant*]: Master Square, or rather Round, farewell.

SERVANT: Good-bye.

[*Exeunt* MARQUIS DE LA MOTA *and servant.*]

DON JUAN [*to Catalinón*]: Follow the Marquis.

CATALINÓN: He has just entered the Alcázar.

DON JUAN: Follow him.

[*Exit* CATALINÓN. *A* WOMAN *speaks behind a barred window.*]

WOMAN: Pst!

DON JUAN: Who's there?

WOMAN: If you are discreet, courteous, and a friend of the Marquis, give him this letter immediately. A lady's happiness depends on it.

Don Juan: I'll give it to him. I am his friend and servant.

Woman: Farewell, stranger.

[*The* Woman *disappears.*]

Don Juan: The voice is gone. Isn't this a fairy tale? The wind was my courier for this letter. Could it be a message from the woman the Marquis was sighing over just now? The playboy of Seville is in luck again! Playboy of Seville! That is what all Spain calls me. The man whose greatest pleasure is to play a woman for a fool and abscond with her honor. By God, now that I've walked away from the square I'll open this! Can she be another Isabela? How delightful! The letter is open. It's hers! Signed, "Doña Ana, your cousin." [*Reads the letter.*] "My cruel father tells me that he has given me away, but not to you. Now as you have given me your pledge of marriage, I entrust myself to you. Come tonight at eleven. You will find a door open. Wear a colored cape. Leonora and my other two servants will let you in, my love. Farewell." Poor lover! Did anyone ever see the likes of this? [*Laughing.*] What a joke. By God, I'll enjoy her through the same lie I used on Isabela in Naples.

[*Enter* Catalinón.]

Catalinón: The Marquis is coming.

Don Juan: We have business tonight.

Catalinón: A new trick?

Don Juan: The best!

Catalinón: I don't approve. We can't go on like this. One of these days you'll be tricked by your own tricks.

Don Juan: You've become a preacher, have you?

Catalinón: Right makes me valiant.

Don Juan: Fear will make you a coward. Since when does a servant have a will of his own? Your duty is to act and keep your mouth shut. And that's my last warning to you.

Catalinón: From now on I'll do as I am told. Say the word and I'll tame a tiger or an elephant.

Don Juan: Quiet, the Marquis is coming.

Catalinón: To be tamed?

[*Enter* Marquis de la Mota.]

Don Juan: Marquis, I was entrusted with a charming message for you through a grill. I couldn't see anyone, but by the voice I understood it was a woman. You are to appear at a certain door at midnight.

The door will be open and all your amorous hopes will be rewarded. But you must wear a colored cape in order to be recognized by little Leonora, the maid.

MARQUIS: What are you saying?

DON JUAN: That I received this message from a window—without seeing a soul.

MARQUIS: Beautiful message! My friend, I owe heaven to you. Let me kiss your feet.

DON JUAN: Remember, I am not your cousin! [*Aside.*] I'm going to make love to her, and you're kissing my feet!

MARQUIS: I'm so happy I've lost my wits. Sun, rush me to her arms!

DON JUAN: It's getting dark already.

MARQUIS: I'm going home at once to get dressed for tonight. I'm absolutely wild.

DON JUAN: Just wait. You'll be even wilder at midnight.

MARQUIS: Best of all cousins—you want to reward my faith and love!

CATALINÓN [*Aside.*]: Christ be my witness, I wouldn't give a penny for his cousin.

[*Exit* MARQUIS DE LA MOTA. *Enter* DON DIEGO TENORIO.]

DON DIEGO: Don Juan.

CATALINÓN: Your father is calling you.

DON JUAN: My lord, what can I do for you?

DON DIEGO: You can become more settled, wiser, and more honorable. Why are you trying to kill me?

DON JUAN: Why do you come to me this way?

DON DIEGO: Because of your behavior, your madness. The King has ordered me to throw you out of the city because of one of your pranks. You concealed it from me, but the King has been informed. Your crime is so serious I hardly dare talk about it. To betray a friend in the royal palace! May God punish you according to your deserts. You fancy that He winks at your crimes, but I say your punishment is at hand. Profaner of God's name, God will be a terrible judge on the day of your death.

DON JUAN: The day of my death? Plenty of time for that. It's a long journey till then.

DON DIEGO: It will seem very short to you then.

DON JUAN: But the journey His Highness requires of me right now, is that a long one too?

DON DIEGO: The King sends you to Lebrija for your treachery—not punishment enough, in my opinion. You will remain there until Duke Octavio is satisfied and the talk in Naples about Isabela has subsided.

CATALINÓN [*Aside.*]: If the old man knew about the poor fishergirl, he'd really foam at the mouth.

DON DIEGO: Since I can't chastize you, say or do what I will, I leave you in the hands of God.

[*Exit* DON DIEGO TENORIO.]

CATALINÓN: The old man was almost crying.

DON JUAN: That's how old people are. Come, it's dark already; let's call on the Marquis.

CATALINÓN: If we must. You've made up your mind to seduce his woman?

DON JUAN: This trick will go down in history.

CATALINÓN: I hope we survive it!

DON JUAN: You're a coward.

CATALINÓN: And you're a regular bluebeard. When you arrive in a town a sign should be posted: "Beware of the great deceiver of women, the playboy of Spain."

DON JUAN: "The playboy of Spain." I like that name.

[*Enter the* MARQUIS DE LA MOTA *and* MUSICIANS, *singing. It is evening.*]

MUSICIAN: Oh what is Love's delight? To hurt each where
          He cares not whom, with darts of deep desire:
          With watchful jealousy, with hope, with fear,
          With nipping cold, and secret flames of fire.*

DON JUAN: What's this?

CATALINÓN: A serenade.

MARQUIS: The words of this song seem meant for me.

DON JUAN: Who is there?

MARQUIS: A friend. Don Juan?

DON JUAN: Is it you, Marquis?

MARQUIS: Who else?

DON JUAN: As soon as I saw your cape I knew it was you.

MARQUIS: Sing, Don Juan is here.

[*The* MUSICIANS *repeat the song.*]

DON JUAN: What's the house you're gazing at?

*From Thomas Watson's "The Shepherd's Solace," in *England's Helicon* (1600). [*Translator's note.*]

MARQUIS: That of Don Gonzalo de Ulloa.

DON JUAN: Well, it's early yet.* Where shall we go?

MARQUIS: To Lisbon.

DON JUAN: But we're in Seville!

MARQUIS: Didn't you know that half the whores of Lisbon live in the best part of Seville?

DON JUAN: Where do they live?

MARQUIS: In Serpent Alley, where the Portuguese Eves tempt our Adams with apples that cost a great deal of money.

CATALINÓN: I don't like the idea of wandering through that street. It's honey in the day but dirt at night. And what Portuguese dirt is like I experienced once when it was slopped over me from a window.

DON JUAN: While you're going to Serpent Alley, I'll have some fun on my side.

MARQUIS: Actually, I've another enterprise waiting for me nearby.

DON JUAN: Why don't you leave that one to me? I'll take care of it for you.

MARQUIS: Good idea. Put on my cape and take my place.

DON JUAN: Excellent. Show me the house.

MARQUIS: Change your voice and accent while you're about it. Do you see that lattice?

DON JUAN: Yes.

MARQUIS: Go up to it, call "Beatrice," and go in.

DON JUAN: What is she like?

MARQUIS: Fresh and plump.

CATALINÓN: Like a water jar.

MARQUIS: We'll meet later by the church.

DON JUAN: Goodbye, Marquis.

[*Exit* MARQUIS DE LA MOTA.]

CATALINÓN: Where to now?

DON JUAN: To my trick.

CATALINÓN: Nobody gets away from you.

DON JUAN: I love these disguises!

CATALINÓN: You threw a cape at the bull.

DON JUAN: No, the poor bull threw it at me!

[*Exeunt* DON JUAN *and* CATALINÓN. *Reenter* MARQUIS DE LA MOTA, *his* SERVANT, *and Musicians.*]

*This sentence, not in the original, has been supplied for the sake of clarity. [*Translator's note.*]

MARQUIS: Beatrice will think it's I calling on her!

SERVANT: Very clever of you.

MARQUIS: I love these errors!

SERVANT: Everything in this world is error.

MARQUIS: My heart beats with the clock. Each quarter of the hour is a step to supreme fulfillment. Oh, it's a cold and frightening night! Come soon, midnight, but after that, let it never be day!

SERVANT: Where is the next party?

MARQUIS: In Serpent Alley.

MUSICIAN: And what shall we sing?

MARQUIS: Anything to flatter my hopes.

MUSICIANS: No sweeter life I try
            Than in her love to die.

[*Exeunt all.*]

DOÑA ANA [*from within*]: Traitor, you are not the Marquis! I'm deceived!

DON JUAN: But I am the Marquis!

DOÑA ANA: Enemy! You lie! You lie!

[*Enter* DON GONZALO, *half-dressed, sword in hand.*]

DON GONZALO: Ana's voice!

DOÑA ANA: Help! Somebody—kill this traitor—he killed my honor!

DON GONZALO: Who could dare? Killed her honor! My God! And her tongue tolling it to the world!

DOÑA ANA: Kill him!

[*Enter* DON JUAN, *sword in hand, and* CATALINÓN.]

DON JUAN: What's here?

DON GONZALO: A gate to the tower of honor, closing in your face.

DON JUAN: Let me pass!

DON GONZALO: First through my sword!

DON JUAN: Listen to me!

DON GONZALO: Don't waste your breath.

DON JUAN: Listen, I say!

DON GONZALO: The cries I heard told me enough.

DON JUAN: I am your nephew!

DON GONZALO: You're lying. The Marquis de la Mota is no traitor. Villain! Your death for my honor!

DON JUAN: I tell you I am the Marquis!

DON GONZALO: And if you are, the offence is all the greater. Traitor, die!

DON JUAN: This is how I die!

[*They fight.*]

CATALINÓN: If I survive this time, no more tricks for me.

DON GONZALO: Oh! You've killed me.

DON JUAN: Blame yourself.

DON GONZALO: What good is life without honor?

DON JUAN [*to Catalinón*]: On our way.

[*Exeunt* DON JUAN *and* CATALINÓN.]

DON GONZALO: Wait! This blood lends me strength. No, he needn't wait. My wrath will follow him. Villainous coward!

[DON GONZALO *is carried off. Enter* MARQUIS DE LA MOTA, *his Servant, and Musicians.*]

MARQUIS: Midnight will be striking soon. It seems to me that Don Juan is taking uncommonly long with Beatrice. Oh the torments of impatience!

[*Reenter* DON JUAN *and* CATALINÓN.]

DON JUAN: Marquis?

MARQUIS: Don Juan?

DON JUAN: Yes. Take back your cape.

MARQUIS: How was the game?

DON JUAN: Sad. Somebody died.

CATALINÓN: And we'd better run away from him.

MARQUIS: But did you trick her?

DON JUAN: Yes, I did.

CATALINÓN [*Aside.*]: And you too, into the bargain.

DON JUAN: But it was a costly joke.

MARQUIS: I'll pay for it, Don Juan, because the woman will blame me for it.

DON JUAN: It's almost twelve.

MARQUIS: May this night last forever the moment I am in Ana's arms.

DON JUAN: Goodbye, Marquis.

CATALINÓN [*Aside.*]: The poor man's due for a surprise.

DON JUAN [*to Catalinón*]: Let's go.

CATALINÓN: I'll be quicker than an eagle.

[*Exeunt* DON JUAN *and* CATALINÓN.]

MARQUIS: You can all go home. I have to proceed alone now.

SERVANT: Night was made for sleep.

[*Exeunt Musicians.*]

VOICES [*Within.*]: Unheard of! Horrible! A calamity!

MARQUIS: God help me! Voices from the Alcázar. At this time? What can it be? I seem to be looking at another burning Troy. Torches like giants of flames. The lights are coming near! Why are they burning like the sun and dividing into squadrons? I must find out before—
[*Enter* DON DIEGO TENORIO *and the Guard.*]

DON DIEGO: Who is there?

MARQUIS: Somebody who wants to know the reason for all this clamor.

DON DIEGO: This is the cape the Commander spoke about in his last words. Arrest him.

MARQUIS: Arrest me? How dare you! I am the Marquis de la Mota!
[*Draws his sword.*]

DON DIEGO: Put up your sword. You can show your courage without using it. The King has ordered your arrest.

MARQUIS: God in heaven!
[*Enter* KING OF CASTILE, *attended.*]

DON DIEGO: My lord, here is the Marquis.

MARQUIS: Your Highness has ordered my arrest?

KING OF CASTILE: Take him and remove him from my presence. I want to see his head on a stake. What! You dare look at me?

MARQUIS: Your highness—my innocence—

KING OF CASTILE: Enough. To the dungeon!

MARQUIS: Oh the tyrannical glories of love, so quick in passing and yet so long in coming. "There's many a slip 'twixt the cup and the lip," says the wise proverb. But why is the King offended? Why am I being arrested?

DON DIEGO: Who knows the answer to that better than you, my lord?

MARQUIS: Than I?

DON DIEGO: Let's go.

MARQUIS: Strange confusion.

KING OF CASTILE: Try the Marquis at once, and off with his head in the morning. As for the Commander's burial, it must be conducted with all the solemnity and dignity he deserves. At my own expense he will be given a tomb and a statue of bronze and matching stone. An inscription in gothic letters will cry out for vengeance. But where did Doña Ana go?

DON DIEGO: To the Queen, my lord, for sanctuary.

KING OF CASTILE: Castile and the rest of the kingdom will mourn this loss; Calatrava will weep the death of a great Commander.
[*Exeunt all.*]

Scene 3

A wedding feast near the village of Dos Hermanas. Enter BATRICIO *and* ARMINTA, GACENO, BELISA, *other* SHEPHERDS *and* MUSICIANS.

MUSICIANS [*singing*]:
> O who can sing her beauties best,
>   or what remains unsung?
> Do thou Apollo tune the rest,
>   unworthy is my tongue.
> To gaze on her, is to be blest,
>   so wondrous fair her face is;
> Her fairness cannot be exprest
>   in Goddesses nor Graces.*

GACENO: Batricio, in giving you my Arminta, I am giving you my soul and my being.

BATRICIO: The meadow puts on its brightest colors for us. I won her with my desires. I deserved her by my labors.

MUSICIANS: A thousand years of union for such a wife and such a husband!

[*They repeat the song.*]

GACENO: Well sung. The Kyrie never sounded better.

BATRICIO: The sun that rises in the east does not rise like the sun of my soul. There is no sun like the sun of her eyes and her brow. My sun shines brighter than the noontide sun. Sing therefore to my sun thousands of sweet melodies.

[*The Musicians repeat the song.*]

ARMINTA: Batricio, I am grateful but you are quite a flatterer. From now on you will be my sun and I will be your moon, and grow by your light alone.

[*Enter a* SHEPHERD.]

SHEPHERD: Gentlemen, you are about to have guests at your wedding feast.

GACENO: Let the whole world participate in our joy.

BATRICIO: Who's coming?

SHEPHERD: Don Juan Tenorio.

BATRICIO: It's an ill wind when a gentleman appears at a feast. I foresee spoiled pleasure and jealousy. How did he hear of my wedding?

SHEPHERD: Traveling on the road to Lebrija.

*From "Theorello: A Shepherd's Idyll" in *England's Helicon*. [*Translator's note.*]

BATRICIO: The devil must have sent him. But why should I worry? Everybody can join us who will. And yet—a gentleman at my wedding—an ill wind for me.

GACENO: Let the whole court of Alfonso the Eleventh come, along with the Colossus of Rhodes, the Pope, and Prester John. They'll find royal entertainment with Gaceno. We have mountains of bread, Guadalquivirs of wine, Babylons of bacon, and larders bursting with birds and doves and basted hens. The presence of this great nobleman among us will be an honor bestowed on my grey head.

SHEPHERD [to Batricio]: Careful. He is the son of the Chamberlain.

BATRICIO: An ill wind for me. They must seat him next to my bride. My pleasure is spoiled and I am jealous already. I'll have to love, suffer, and be still.

[Enter DON JUAN and CATALINÓN in traveling clothes.]

DON JUAN: I heard on the highway of a wedding here. I should like to join in your festivities, since I was fortunate enough to hear about them.

GACENO: You have come to honor and magnify them.

BATRICIO [Aside.]: I am in charge here and I still say you've come in an evil hour.

GACENO: Give the gentleman a seat.

DON JUAN: If you allow me, I'll sit here.

[He sits next to ARMINTA.]

BATRICIO: But if you sit before me, sir, you'll be taking the bridegroom's place.

DON JUAN: That doesn't sound too bad.

GACENO: He is the bridegroom, sir.

DON JUAN: Forgive my error and ignorance.

BATRICIO [Aside.]: Why must I always be the loser?

CATALINÓN [Aside.]: Poor fellow, he's fallen into Lucifer's hands.

DON JUAN [to Arminta]: Is it possible, madam, that I should be so fortunate? I really envy your husband.

ARMINTA: You seem to be a flatterer.

BATRICIO [Aside.]: I was right. Nobility at a wedding is an ill wind that blows no good.

DON JUAN: Your hands are too delicate to grant to a peasant.

CATALINÓN [Aside.]: Give him your hand in game and you'll lose your hand in earnest.

BATRICIO [Aside.]: Jealousy will kill me.

GACENO: Let's eat now to give our new friend a chance to rest.

Don Juan [*to Arminta*]: Why do you hide your hand?

Arminta: It doesn't belong to me.

Gaceno: Sing, everybody!

Don Juan [*to Catalinón*]: What do you think of all this?

Catalinón [*to Don Juan*]: These bumpkins may massacre us yet.

Don Juan: Beautiful eyes and delicate hands—they have set me on fire.

Catalinón: Time to brand another lamb. This makes four.

Don Juan: Come, they're watching me.

Batricio [*Aside.*]: Didn't I say it was an ill wind?

Gaceno: Sing! Sing!

Batricio [*Aside.*]: I'm dying!

Catalinón: Sing now, cry later.

[*The Musicians repeat the song.*]

ACT III

Scene 1

Gaceno's house in the village of Dos Hermanas. Enter Batricio, *deep in thought.*

Batricio: Oh Jealousy, my death and my hell, spare me! I am worn out with rage and grief. And he, the great man, why does he torment me? What does he want? I was right when I cried, "It's an ill wind" after seeing him. Not only must he sit next to my wife, but he wouldn't allow me to dip a finger into my own plate! He brushed my hand aside every time I tried to taste a dish. "Tut, tut, such bad manners!" he said. And he stuck so close to Arminta that people began to think he was her husband, and I his best man. When I wanted to speak with my own bride, he growled, "Such bad manners" again and shoved me aside. And when I appealed to the others they just smiled and answered, "You have no reason to complain. It really is nothing. What are you afraid of? Keep quiet, it must be a custom at court." Custom devil! It may have been a custom in Sodom for a stranger to eat of the bridal dish while the bridegroom went hungry! And the other rascal, each time I got my hands on something to eat, he'd say, "You don't like this? You really have no taste for finer things," and suddenly take it away from me. I'm simply furious! Is this a wedding or a practical joke? Am I among Christians? Now that supper is over, I suppose he will follow us to bed too. And when I hug my wife, he'll say, "Tut, tut, such bad manners!" Here he comes. What shall I do? I can't stand it—I'll hide. Too late—he saw me.

[*Enter* DON JUAN.]

DON JUAN: Batricio.

BATRICIO: At your service, sir.

DON JUAN: When love rages in the soul, Batricio, it will speak out. I must tell you—

BATRICIO [*Aside.*]: Another calamity for me?

DON JUAN: Some time ago I gave my heart to Arminta, and I enjoyed . . .

BATRICIO: Her honor?

DON JUAN: Yes.

BATRICIO [*Aside.*]: This confirms what my own eyes have seen. If Arminta didn't love him she would never have allowed me to be insulted so.

DON JUAN: I have been her promised husband, and have enjoyed her favors, these six months. I tell you this because I see no other way out. But I speak the truth, Batricio. Our engagement and our friendship were kept secret because of the King and my father. But neither reason nor law can keep two loving souls apart. Don't stand in the way of our marriage, my friend. Either I must be satisfied, or else, by God, I'll kill whoever has given me trouble.

BATRICIO: Since you're allowing me to choose, my lord, I'll do as you like. Gossip is the ruin of honor and women. A woman's reputation is like a bell; one crack in it, and it's broken for good. Enjoy her, my lord, enjoy her a thousand years. I'd rather die with the truth than live with a lie.

[*Exit* BATRICIO.]

DON JUAN: I vanquished him by appealing to honor. These peasants are always consulting their honor, as though they carried it in their hands. And no wonder. After so many deceptions, honor has fled from the city to the countryside. So then: I twisted him around my little finger, and now I can enjoy the girl without fear. Night is falling, and I have yet to hoodwink her father. Stars in the sky, look down upon me and, if I am not to be punished till the day of my death, grant me luck in this hoax!

[*Exit* DON JUAN. *Enter* ARMINTA *and* BELISA.]

BELISA: Arminta, your bridegroom is coming. Time to go into the house and get undressed.

ARMINTA: Belisa, I don't know what to think of this unhappy wedding. Who is this gentleman who deprives me of my joy? My poor Batricio was drowning in melancholy all day; I saw him jealous and perplexed. So much misfortune! I hate the man who separates me from my love. Shameless impudence has become a mark of nobility in Spain. Leave me now, Belisa; I don't know what to think. I feel lost. Go now. I hate the man who separates me from my love. . . .

BELISA: Go in; I think I hear Batricio coming. It couldn't be anyone else in the house of newlyweds.

ARMINTA: Good night, my dear Belisa.

BELISA: Comfort him in your arms.

ARMINTA: God, turn my sighs into words of love, my tears into caresses. [*Exeunt* BELISA *and* ARMINTA. *Enter* DON JUAN, GACENO *and* CATALINÓN.]

DON JUAN: God be with you, Gaceno.

GACENO: I'd like to come with you to inform my daughter of her good fortune.

DON JUAN: That can wait till tomorrow.

GACENO: You're right. In giving you my daughter, Don Juan, I am giving my soul away.

DON JUAN: Your daughter is now my wife.

[*Exit* GACENO.]

DON JUAN: Saddle the mares, Catalinón.

CATALINÓN: When do we leave?

DON JUAN: At dawn, and dying with laughter after this trick.

CATALINÓN: Master, another wedding is waiting for us in Lebrija, so hurry with this one.

DON JUAN: This is going to be my most refined hoax.

CATALINÓN: Excellent; but see we don't get hoaxed right back, and that we come out of this merrymaking alive.

DON JUAN: What are you afraid of? Isn't my father the Chief Justice, and isn't he the King's favorite?

CATALINÓN: God punishes favorites too when they wink at evildoing. And at the gambling table it can happen that those who just look on also get hurt. God knows I've looked on at your games, but I don't care to be reduced to cinders by a bolt from heaven, not me!

DON JUAN: Enough—saddle the mares. Tomorrow we'll sleep in Seville.

CATALINÓN: In Seville?

DON JUAN: Yes.

CATALINÓN: You're joking! Think of what you did in Seville! Remember there's only a little step from the longest life to death, and from death to hell.

DON JUAN: If you give me that much time, come, deceits, come, pranks!

CATALINÓN: Sir . . . !

DON JUAN: Go on, your cowardice bores me.

[*Exit* CATALINÓN.]

DON JUAN: Night spreads out its dark silence, and the Pleiades tread the highest pole among clusters of stars. Now is the time for adventure. Love, whom no man can resist, be my guide to her bed. Arminta!

ARMINTA: Who's calling me? My Batricio?

DON JUAN: I am not Batricio.

ARMINTA: Then who is it?

DON JUAN: Look carefully, Arminta.

ARMINTA: My God, I am ruined! In my room at this hour!

DON JUAN: This hour is mine, Arminta.

ARMINTA: Leave at once, or I'll shout for help. You owe Batricio some courtesy. We too in our village have our Emilias and our Lucretias.

DON JUAN: Arminta, two words! Listen to me and conceal your warm, your precious blush in your heart.

ARMINTA: Leave me, my husband is coming.

DON JUAN: I am your husband. Are you surprised?

ARMINTA: Since when?

DON JUAN: Since now.

ARMINTA: Who settled this?

DON JUAN: My good fortune.

ARMINTA: Does Batricio know?

DON JUAN: Yes; he has forgotten you.

ARMINTA: Forgotten me?

DON JUAN: Yes, because I adore you.

ARMINTA: Adore me?

DON JUAN: In these two arms.

ARMINTA: Leave!

DON JUAN: How can I? I would die without you.

ARMINTA: You lie!

DON JUAN: Arminta, listen to the truth—for are not women friends of truth? I am a nobleman, heir to the ancient family of the Tenorios, the conquerors of Seville. After the King, my father is the most powerful and considered man at court. His lips hold power of life and death. By chance I happened on this road and saw you. Love sometimes behaves in a manner that surprises even himself. I saw you, adored you, and love burns in me so, that I must marry you. Let the King disapprove, my father forbid and threaten, and the whole kingdom murmur, yet I will be your husband. Batricio has foregone his rights, and your father has sent me here to give you my hand in marriage. Speak to me now, Arminta.

ARMINTA: I don't know if what you're saying is truth or lying rhetoric. I am married to Batricio, everybody knows it. How can the marriage be annulled, even if he abandons me?

DON JUAN: When the marriage is not consummated, whether by malice or deceit, it can be annulled.

ARMINTA: You are right. But, God help me, won't you desert me the moment you have separated me from my husband? With Batricio all was simple truth.

DON JUAN: Come! Give me your hand and confirm your pledge to me.

ARMINTA: You're not deceiving me?

DON JUAN: To deceive you would be to deceive myself.

ARMINTA: Then swear that you will carry out your promise.

DON JUAN: By your white hand: I swear.

ARMINTA: Call on God to damn you if you are untrue.

DON JUAN: If I do not keep my word, let God send a man to ensnare and kill me. [*Aside.*] A dead man, of course. God forbid he should be alive.

ARMINTA: With this oath, I am your wife.

DON JUAN: My soul is yours.

ARMINTA: Yours are my soul and my life.

DON JUAN: Arminta, light of my eyes, tomorrow your beautiful feet will slip into polished silver slippers with buttons of the purest gold. And your alabaster throat will be imprisoned in beautiful necklaces; on your fingers, rings set with amethysts will shine like stars, and from your ears will dangle oriental pearls.

ARMINTA: I am yours.

DON JUAN [*Aside.*]: Little you know the playboy of Seville!
[*Exeunt.*]

Scene 2

Near Tarragona. Enter DUCHESS ISABELA *and* FABIO, *her companion.*

FABIO: Isabela, what good is sadness? It is true that love is a deceiver; he attacks those who were laughing at him; and presently they weep.

His gifts are torment, fear, suffering, and scorn. And when you left Naples, your suffering was understandable. But now you can exchange grief for joy. A new day is breaking for you. You lost Octavio, but Don Juan awaits you to take your beautiful hand, and your happiness will not be long delayed. Hold back your tears and your complaints—his house is one of the best of Castile.

ISABELA: I do not grieve because I am to marry Don Juan. The whole world knows his rank. What I weep, and must weep forever, is my lost reputation, the tale of which has spread wherever I go.

FABIO: Soon you'll be in his arms, tenderly entwined, like the ivy and the elm.

ISABELA: Even in my bridal bed I will remember my honor lost and my reputation ruined.

FABIO: Isabela, look at that fishergirl. She is sitting on a rock, gazing at the sea, crying softly and addressing her complaints to the sky. Listen! She is asking for vengeance; she is mourning the loss of something precious, and of hope. I'll ask her to keep you company while I look after the rest of our escort. Tell her your griefs. Take ease together with sweet laments.

[*He leaves.*]

ISABELA: A traitor robbed me of my beloved master and my dearest treasure. Oh bitter night, mask of the sun and mask of truth!

[*Enter* TISBEA.]

TISBEA: Violent Spanish sea—torrents of water and flying waves, carrying to the coast now innocent shells, now bitter deceit. You know my lament, for you bore my miseries. I cry into your deaf ears. You destroyed my honor—the honor of Tisbea, known for her cruelty to men!

ISABELA: Beautiful fishermaid, why do you complain so bitterly of the sea?

TISBEA: It nursed my ruin. You who are fortunate can look on it and smile.

ISABELA: I, too, weep because of the sea.

TISBEA: Why? Has a ravisher forced you with him across it, like a second Europa?

ISABELA: They are taking me to Seville to be married against my wishes.

TISBEA: Then you will understand my plight and pity my tears. Listen. The waters washed ashore a man named Don Juan Tenorio; victim of a shipwreck, and dying. I nursed him back to health and made him a guest in my house. But the guest turned viper in my nest, lied to me, deceived me, gave me his pledge of marriage, and with sweet false words robbed me of my honor, and left me after enjoying me.

ISABELA: Enough! Cursed woman! Out of my sight! Oh, you have killed me. No, wait, if it was grief that moved you, you are not to blame. Continue. Is it all true?

TISBEA: True as life and death.

ISABELA: Evil strike the woman who believes the words of a man! It was God who brought me to this hut. You have revived my determination to seek revenge. Evil strike the woman who believes the words of a man!

TISBEA: I beg you to take me with you, my lady, and my poor old father as well. He wants to ask the King for justice and satisfaction. And Anfriso, the man I should have married and loved forever, and who wants me even now, let him come with us too.

ISABELA: You may all come with me.

TISBEA: Evil strike the woman who believes the words of a man!

[*Exeunt.*]

Scene 3

Inside a church in Seville. Enter DON JUAN *and* CATALINÓN.

CATALINÓN: Everything is going wrong.

DON JUAN: Why?

CATALINÓN: Octavio has found out about the matter in Italy. The Marquis is complaining to the King that you fooled him with a false message from his cousin and that you borrowed his cape to ruin him. They say that Isabela is coming over to be your wife. They say—

DON JUAN [*cuffing him*]: Enough!

CATALINÓN: You broke one of my teeth!

DON JUAN: Tattler! Who told you all this nonsense?

CATALINÓN: Nonsense?

DON JUAN: Yes, nonsense.

CATALINÓN: It's all true.

DON JUAN: I don't care. Let Octavio try to kill me. Am I dead? Don't I have two good hands? Come, where did you find us a room?

CATALINÓN: In a secluded street.

DON JUAN: Fine.

CATALINÓN: Meantime this church can be your sanctuary.

DON JUAN: Why don't you tell me next they'll kill me here in broad daylight? Come—did you see the bridegroom of Dos Hermanas?

CATALINÓN: Yes. Full of anguish, too.

DON JUAN: Arminta won't discover our hoax for two weeks.

CATALINÓN: She is so blind to it that she calls herself Doña Arminta.

DON JUAN: This is going to be delicious.

CATALINÓN: Of course. But she'll cry for it.

[*They see the tomb of Don Gonzalo de Ulloa.*]

DON JUAN: Whose tomb is this?

CATALINÓN: Don Gonzalo's.

DON JUAN: The man I killed! Quite a tomb!

CATALINÓN: That's how the King ordered it. What does the inscription say?

DON JUAN [*reading*]: "Here the most loyal of knights expects God's vengeance on a traitor." [*He laughs. To the Statue*] So you want vengeance, old boy, stone-beard!

[DON JUAN *pulls the Statue's beard.*]

CATALINÓN: You can't pluck it—he has a powerful beard.

DON JUAN [*to the Statue*]: Join me tonight for supper at my inn. We can fight it out there and then, if you're still hungry for vengeance. Of course, I can't promise you a good scuffle if you carry a stone sword in your hand.

CATALINÓN: Well, if he's coming to dine with us, let's go order a meal.

DON JUAN [*to the Statue*]: You've been waiting a long time for this vengeance. If you still want it, you'd better wake from your sleep. Or are you waiting for me to die? If you are, give up hoping, because I've plenty of time till then, plenty of time.

[*Exeunt* DON JUAN *and* CATALINÓN.]

Scene 4

An inn in Seville. Enter two SERVANTS. *They set a table.*

FIRST SERVANT: Let's prepare supper. Don Juan should be coming soon.

SECOND SERVANT: The table is ready. But what made him order an early supper? He usually comes in at dawn.

FIRST SERVANT: I suppose he wants more time for his gallivanting tonight.

[*Enter* DON JUAN *and* CATALINÓN.]

DON JUAN [*to Catalinón*]: Did you lock the door?

CATALINÓN: Just as you ordered.

DON JUAN [*to the Servants*]: Quick! Fetch my dinner!

SECOND SERVANT: It is here already.

DON JUAN: Catalinón, sit down!

CATALINÓN: I really prefer to eat alone.

DON JUAN: I told you: sit down.

CATALINÓN: I am sitting.

FIRST SERVANT [*Aside*.]: He must think he's on the road, to eat with his valet.

[*A knock*.]

CATALINÓN: Quite a knock!

DON JUAN: See who's at the door.

FIRST SERVANT: I'll open.

CATALINÓN: It could be the constables, master.

DON JUAN: Let them come; no reason to worry.

[*The* FIRST SERVANT *runs back in fright*.]

FIRST SERVANT: My God, what I've seen!

DON JUAN [*to First Servant*]: Speak, what happened? What did you see?

CATALINÓN: He looks a little scared.

DON JUAN: Did you see a devil or what? I'm getting angry.

[*More knocks*.]

CATALINÓN: They're knocking again!

DON JUAN [*to Catalinón*]: You'd better go see who it is.

CATALINÓN: Who? Me?

DON JUAN: Yes, you. Move!

CATALINÓN: Listen, master. My grandmother was found hanging like a bunch of grapes—and since then they say she wanders over the earth like a soul in pain. That's why I don't like all this knocking.

DON JUAN: Enough!

CATALINÓN: Master, you know I am a coward.

DON JUAN: The door!

CATALINÓN: I'm sick.

DON JUAN: Still standing?

CATALINÓN: Who has the keys?

SECOND SERVANT: The door is only bolted.

DON JUAN: What's wrong? Why don't you go?

CATALINÓN: This marks the end of Catalinón. The seduced women have come to take their revenge on the two of us.

[CATALINÓN *goes to the door and comes running back*.]

DON JUAN: What now?

CATALINÓN: God help me! They're killing me; they caught me!

DON JUAN: Who's caught you? And who's killing you? What did you see?

CATALINÓN: Master, when I . . . got there . . . I saw . . . I ran back . . .

Who grabbed me? Who pulled me? I arrived . . . I was blinded
. . . When I saw him . . . I swear to God! He spoke and said, "Who
are you? . . ." he answered . . . and I answered . . . and then . . . I
ran into and saw . . .

DON JUAN: Saw what?

CATALINÓN: I don't know.

DON JUAN: Is this what wine does to you? Give me the light, chicken,
and I'll see for myself.

[DON JUAN *takes the candle and moves toward the door. The* STATUE
OF DON GONZALO *comes to meet him.* DON JUAN *falls back, dismayed,
his hand on his sword. Slowly, the* STATUE *comes closer to* DON JUAN,
*who retreats until the two are standing face to face at the center of
the stage.*]

DON JUAN: Who are you?

THE STATUE: It is I.

DON JUAN: Who?

THE STATUE: The man you invited to dinner.

DON JUAN: To dinner, then! And if you brought friends they'll find
plenty to eat too. The table is set. Sit down.

CATALINÓN: Angels protect me!

DON JUAN: Catalinón, sit next to the dead man.

CATALINÓN: I already had supper. You go ahead with your guest. I
don't think I can eat a thing just now.

DON JUAN: You're a fool. Are you afraid of a dead man? What would
you do if he were alive? Base and stupid fear!

CATALINÓN: I am really bloated.

DON JUAN: I'll get angry, watch out!

CATALINÓN: Excuse me, sir, but I smell bad.

DON JUAN: Sit down! I'm waiting for you.

CATALINÓN: I can't. My—uh—posterior has died on me.

DON JUAN [*to the Servants*]: And you fools, why do you stand there
trembling?

CATALINÓN: I never liked to eat with foreigners. And now you force
me to eat with a guest made out of stone.

DON JUAN: What can a man of stone do to you?

CATALINÓN: Break my head, for instance.

DON JUAN: Why don't you speak to him? Politely, now.

CATALINÓN [*to the Statue*]: How are you? Are you well lodged—in the
great beyond? Does it have many mountains or is it flat? Do they appreciate poetry there?

FIRST SERVANT: He nods to everything.

CATALINÓN: Are there many taverns? There must be, if Noah lives there.

DON JUAN [to the Servants]: You there, something to drink!

CATALINÓN: Sir Dead Man, in this country of yours, do they mix their drinks with ice? [The STATUE nods.] With ice. Good country.

DON JUAN [to the Statue]: If you'd like some singing, they'll sing. [The STATUE nods.]

SECOND SERVANT: He said yes!

DON JUAN: Sing!

CATALINÓN: Sir Deadly has good taste. He is a nobleman, and fond of merriment.

[Singing within.]

> Lady, take me as I am,
>   A man of rich desires.
> Youth is mine, and I shall live
>   To light a thousand fires.

CATALINÓN: This Sir Corpse isn't eating much. It's either the summer weather or simply that he is a man with a small appetite. I can't keep my hands from shaking. They must drink little over there—but I'll drink for two. [He drinks.] A toast to stone! By God, I feel better already.

[Singing within.]

> Lady, take me as I am,
>   A man of rich desires.
> Youth is mine, and I shall live
>   To light a thousand fires.
>
> Do not speak of death to me,
>   Lady, I shall never learn.
> Life is long, my credit sound,
>   I must love before I burn.

CATALINON: Which one of your seduced ladies are they singing about, master?

DON JUAN: Tonight I laugh at them all. Back in Naples, Isabela—

CATALINÓN: That one isn't really cheated now, master, since she is to be your wife, as is right. But you cheated the fishergirl who saved you from the sea, and paid her with counterfeit coin for her hospitality. Next you seduced Doña Ana—

DON JUAN: Quiet! Here's her would-be avenger who suffered for her.

CATALINÓN: Of course, he is a very brave man. And he is made of stone, and you of flesh and blood. Not a pleasant situation.

[*The* STATUE *signals that it wants to be alone with* DON JUAN.]

DON JUAN: You two, clear the table! He wants to remain alone with me.

CATALINÓN: Bad sign! Don't stay with him. Dead people can often kill a giant with a single bite.

DON JUAN: Out, all of you! I'm not Catalinón! Go, he is coming closer to me.

[*Exeunt* SERVANTS *and* CATALINÓN.]

DON JUAN: The door is shut. I'm waiting. What do you want, oh shadow, phantom, or vision? If you walk in torment or if you are seeking satisfaction, tell me, and I give you my word that I shall do whatever you command. Do you enjoy God's grace, or is your soul damned? Did I kill you in a state of mortal sin? Speak, I am anxious to hear you.

THE STATUE [*speaking slowly as if from another world*]: Will you keep your word as a gentleman?

DON JUAN: I am a man of honor and I keep my word.

THE STATUE: Give me your hand, then. Don't be afraid.

DON JUAN: What? I afraid? Were you Hell itself, I would give you my hand.

THE STATUE: I have your hand and your word. I shall look for you tomorrow night. I will offer you supper at ten o'clock. Will you come?

DON JUAN: I expected something more challenging. Tomorrow I'll be your guest. Where do we meet?

THE STATUE: In my chapel.

DON JUAN: Shall I come alone?

THE STATUE: No, both of you come. But keep your word as I have kept mine.

DON JUAN: I will keep it. I am a Tenorio.

THE STATUE: And I, Ulloa.

DON JUAN: I shan't fail.

THE STATUE: I believe you. Adieu.

[*It moves toward the door.*]

DON JUAN: Wait, I'll give you a light.

THE STATUE: I need no light. I am in grace.

[*The* STATUE *leaves very slowly, watching* DON JUAN. DON JUAN *remains alone and shaken.*]

DON JUAN: God help me! My body is soaked with sweat and my heart is frozen in my body. When he took my hand, he burnt it with a hellish heat unlike any living warmth. And as he spoke, his breath blew like an infernal wind. Pah! I must be imagining all this: fear of the dead is the basest of all fears. If I don't cower before the noblest men alive, powerful men, reasonable and endowed with souls, why should I tremble before a dead body? Tomorrow I shall be his guest in the chapel. All Seville will be terrified and astounded by my courage. [*Exit* DON JUAN.]

Scene 5

A room in the Alcázar in Seville. Enter the KING OF CASTILE *and* DON DIEGO TENORIO.

KING OF CASTILE: Has Isabela arrived?

DON DIEGO: Yes, but dissatisfied.

KING OF CASTILE: Isn't she happy about this marriage?

DON DIEGO: Her reputation is ruined.

KING OF CASTILE: But her anguish stems from something else, surely. Where is she?

DON DIEGO: At the convent of the Carmelites.

KING OF CASTILE: Let her leave the convent at once. I want her here at the palace. She will wait on the Queen.

DON DIEGO: If she is to marry Don Juan, Your Highness should command his presence at court.

KING OF CASTILE: Let him come. I want the news of their marriage to be spread to the whole world. Tomorrow Don Juan will be Count of Lebrija. He will own it and rule it. Isabela loved and lost a duke but gained a count.

DON DIEGO: We all acknowledge your bounty.

KING OF CASTILE: I owe you so many favors that even with this I remain behind in my payments. Don Diego, what do you think of marrying Doña Ana today as well?

DON DIEGO: To Octavio?

KING OF CASTILE: No, Duke Octavio cannot be the one to undo the wrong. Doña Ana has pleaded with me by intermediary of the Queen to forgive the Marquis. Now that her father is dead she wants a husband. In the Marquis she will find both a husband and a father. Don Diego, go quietly with a few people to speak with him at the Fortress of Triana, and inform him that I pardon him for the welfare and security of his cousin.

DON DIEGO: Again, I see my wishes fulfilled.

KING OF CASTILE: You can tell him they will be married tonight.

DON DIEGO: All ends well. It will be easy to persuade the Marquis—he is devoted to his cousin.

KING OF CASTILE: You should also inform Octavio. The Duke has no luck with women. Poor man, they are only interested in appearances and talk. By the way, I hear that he is very angry with your son.

DON DIEGO: I daresay he found out that he owes his misfortunes to Don Juan. Look—here he is.

KING OF CASTILE: Don't leave my side. Your son's crime touches you too. [*Enter* OCTAVIO.]

OCTAVIO: Unconquerable King, allow me to kiss your feet.

KING OF CASTILE: Rise, Duke, and cover your head. What is your wish?

OCTAVIO: I have come to kneel at your feet with a just suit, worthy of being granted.

KING OF CASTILE: Duke, if it is just, I give you my word: it will be granted. Speak!

OCTAVIO: My lord, you have learned by letters from your Ambassador, and the rumor has reached everyone, that one night in Naples—an evil night for me—Don Juan Tenorio used my name with Spanish arrogance to violate the honor of a lady.

KING OF CASTILE: Enough! I know your disgrace. What is it exactly you want?

OCTAVIO: Permission to prove him a traitor in the field.

DON DIEGO: You will not! His blood is noble—

KING OF CASTILE: Don Diego!

DON DIEGO: My lord.

OCTAVIO: Who are you to speak like this to the King?

DON DIEGO: One who keeps silent at the King's command. Or I would answer you with this sword.

OCTAVIO: You're old.

DON DIEGO: In Italy I was young once—as you Italians found out to your sorrow. My sword was familiar to Naples and Milan.

OCTAVIO: But now your blood is frozen. *Is* is what matters, not *was*.

DON DIEGO: I *was* and I *am*.

KING OF CASTILE: Stop! Enough! Be still, Don Diego! You are showing little respect for my person. And you, Duke Octavio, you will be able to speak at your leisure after the weddings. Don Juan is a gentleman of my house, and of my making, and [*pointing to* DON DIEGO] he is a branch of that venerable trunk. Respect him as such.

OCTAVIO: My lord, I will do as you say.

KING OF CASTILE: Follow me, Don Diego.

DON DIEGO [*Aside.*]: Oh, my son! How poorly you have repaid the love I have given you.*

[*Exeunt* KING OF CASTILE *and* DON DIEGO.]

OCTAVIO: Is there a man as wretched as I in this world? I trusted in a treacherous friend. I was accused in his place by Isabela because she had lost her dearest jewel, her reputation. But if the King will not avenge her, I, Octavio, will.

[*Enter* GACENO *and* ARMINTA.]

GACENO: This gentleman will tell us where to find Don Juan Tenorio. [*To Octavio*] Sir, could you tell us where to find a Don Juan whose name, I am sure, is well known at court?

OCTAVIO: I suppose you mean Don Juan Tenorio?

ARMINTA: Yes, that's the one.

OCTAVIO: He is here. Do you want to see him?

ARMINTA: I do. He is my husband.

OCTAVIO: What?

ARMINTA: You haven't heard about it here at the Alcázar?

OCTAVIO: Don Juan hasn't said anything to me.

GACENO: Is that possible?

OCTAVIO: I assure you.

GACENO: Doña Arminta is an honorable woman. We are an old family, Christian to the bones. Besides, she is the sole heir to our farm, better than a count or a marquis. Don Juan promised to marry her, and took her away from Batricio.

ARMINTA: Tell him I was a virgin when Don Juan took me.

GACENO: That's beside the point.

OCTAVIO [*Aside.*]: Here is another of Don Juan's pranks. And I'll be able to use what they've told me for my vengeance. [*Aloud.*] What can I do for you?

GACENO: Well, the days are going by, and I would like the ceremony to be performed. If not, I'll take the matter to the King.

OCTAVIO: Your demands are just.

GACENO: Also reasonable and lawful.

OCTAVIO [*Aside.*]: This couldn't have fallen out better! [*Aloud.*] A wedding is being prepared in the Alcázar just now.

---

*Three lines are omitted here, in which the King promises Octavio that his marriage will take place tomorrow. As Ana has been promised to the Marquis, and Isabela to Don Juan, either the King is soothing Octavio with a regal lie, or—more likely—Tirso slipped. [*Translator's note.*]

ARMINTA: Maybe it's mine!

OCTAVIO [*Aside.*]: A little stratagem is called for at this point. [*Aloud.*] Come, my lady. You shall be dressed as befits a lady of the court, and then I myself shall lead you into the King's apartment.

ARMINTA: And take me by the hand to Don Juan, too.

OCTAVIO: A cunning idea.

GACENO: I like your plan, sir.

OCTAVIO [*Aside.*]: With these two, my revenge is set. Isabela, you shall be satisfied.

[*Exeunt all.*]

Scene 6

The Fortress of Triana. Enter DON DIEGO TENORIO *and* MARQUIS DE LA MOTA.

DON DIEGO [*to a Guard*]: Release the Marquis.

MARQUIS: If I am going to my death, I wish to thank you.

DON DIEGO: The King has ordered your release.

MARQUIS: Does he know my innocence? Has he recognized the man who is really guilty—and whose name I refrain from speaking for your sake?

DON DIEGO: For my sake! First you kill your uncle and then you blame me!

MARQUIS: I blame you for accusing me. Your son killed him. I gave Don Juan my cape. False villain! I was about to die for nothing.

DON DIEGO: What are you saying?

MARQUIS: Nothing but the truth. Don Juan took a message from my cousin, addressed to me. It was an invitation—to enjoy her at eleven o'clock that night. But the villain told me midnight, and at eleven he entered her room in my place. I mourn for my uncle, but oh, the greater misery is that Don Juan took my cousin from me, and held her in his arms!

[*Exeunt.*]

Scene 7

Before the church. Enter DON JUAN *and* CATALINÓN.

CATALINÓN: How did the King receive you?

DON JUAN: More affectionately than my father.

CATALINÓN: Did you see Isabela?

Don Juan: Yes.

Catalinón: How is she?

Don Juan: Like an angel.

Catalinón: Did she receive you well?

Don Juan: She turned pale, and then she blushed—like a rose bursting out of its petals at dawn.

Catalinón: Is the wedding set for tonight?

Don Juan: Without fail.

Catalinón: Had you married before, master, you wouldn't have had time to seduce so many women. As it is, you're taking a wife with troubles on all sides.

Don Juan: Again talking like a fool?

Catalinón: Why can't you get married tomorrow? Today is a bad day.

Don Juan: Why?

Catalinón: It's Tuesday.*

Don Juan: Fool. The only bad day for me is when I'm short of cash. Everything else is nonsense.

Catalinón: Come sir, you have to get dressed. It's late and they'll be waiting for you.

Don Juan: First we have another business to settle.

Catalinón: Like what?

Don Juan: Dining with the dead man.

Catalinón: Folly of all follies!

Don Juan: I gave my word.

Catalinón: What if you break it! I don't see what recourse a man of stone has.

Don Juan: He could slander me.

Catalinón: The church is closed anyway.

Don Juan: Knock.

Catalinón: I don't see why. Who's going to open? The sacristans are asleep.

Don Juan: Knock at this little door.

Catalinón: It's open!

Don Juan: Well, go in.

Catalinón: Let a monk sprinkle the place first with holy water.

Don Juan: Be quiet and follow me.

Catalinón: I should be quiet?

---

*Tuesdays and Fridays were considered bad days for traveling or getting married. [*Translator's note.*]

Don Juan: Yes.

Catalinón: God deliver me from these dinners.

[*They enter through a door.*]

Catalinón: How dark the church is and yet so large! Oh God! Master, hold me, somebody is pulling me by the cape!

[*Enter the* Statue of Don Gonzalo.]

Don Juan: Who is there?

The Statue: It is I.

Catalinón: Now I'm done for.

The Statue: I am the dead man; don't be afraid. I did not think you would keep your word, Don Juan—since you make a joke of everything.

Don Juan: You consider me a coward?

The Statue: Yes, I do, for on a certain night you fled after killing me.

Don Juan: Only because I didn't want to be recognized. But now I am here. What do you want?

The Statue: I want to invite you to supper.

Catalinón: You must excuse us. We have no taste for cold dishes, and I don't even see a kitchen.

Don Juan: I accept.

The Statue: But first you must lift the lid of this tomb.

Don Juan: I will lift these pillars too, if you like.

The Statue: You are very brave.

Don Juan: I'm full of life and strength.

Catalinón: A black table! Don't you have anyone to wash it?

The Statue: Sit down.

Don Juan: Where?

Catalinón: Here come two black servants with stools.

[*Enter two Figures in black carrying stools. They set the table.*]

The Statue [*to Catalinón*]: Sit down, too.

Catalinón: Excuse me, sir, I have already eaten. Dine with your guest.

Don Juan: Stop your chatter.

Catalinón: I stop. God, help me out of this broil. What kind of dish is this?

The Statue: Vipers and scorpions.

Catalinón: Such delicacies!

The Statue: These are our specialties. [*To Don Juan*] Aren't you eating?

Don Juan: I would eat if you fed me all the vipers of hell.

Catalinón: What kind of wine do you drink in the hereafter?

THE STATUE: Try some!

CATALINÓN: Pah! Gall and vinegar!

THE STATUE: Such is the wine from our cellars. Now listen to a song.

VOICES:
> Fool, think not that Heaven
>   Can forget a crime.
> God exacts full payment
>   In his own due time.
> There shall no sinner boast,
>   While mocking God's command,
> "Life is long, there's time to pay."
>   Sinner, judgment is at hand!

CATALINÓN: A foul song, by Jesus! Did you hear it, master? It was meant for you.

DON JUAN: My blood is freezing up.

CATALINÓN: Try a little of this ragout.

DON JUAN: I have eaten. Tell them to take away the table.

THE STATUE: Give me your hand. Never fear; give me your hand.

DON JUAN: Fear? Take it! . . . Ai, I'm burning alive! Burning, burning!

THE STATUE: This is little compared to the fire you were looking for. The wonders of God, Don Juan, are unfathomable. His justice demands that a dead man exact the payment of your crimes. As a man sows, so shall he reap.

DON JUAN: I'm burning, let my hand go! [DON JUAN *draws his dagger with his free hand.*] I'll stab you to death. . . . Useless! I'm stabbing the empty air!

THE STATUE: Don Juan! You are paying for the women you cheated.

DON JUAN: I didn't harm your daughter! She saw the hoax in time.

THE STATUE: No matter! Your intention condemns you.

DON JUAN: Let me send for a priest at least; I want to confess and be absolved!

THE STATUE: It cannot be. You thought of that too late.

DON JUAN: I'm burning, burning! I'm dying!

[DON JUAN *dies.*]

CATALINÓN: No escaping. I see I'm going to die too for following you about.

THE STATUE: This is the justice of God. As a man sows, so shall he reap.

[*A great noise. The tomb sinks with* DON JUAN *and* STATUE OF DON GONZALO. CATALINÓN *crawls on the ground.*]

CATALINÓN: God in heaven! What's happening? The whole chapel is burning; and I'm left here for the wake. If I can crawl out of here I'll tell his father. Saint George, Saint Agnus Dei, get me out into the street alive!

Scene 8

A room in the Alcázar in Seville. Enter KING OF CASTILE, DON DIEGO, *and courtiers.*

DON DIEGO: My lord, the Marquis wishes to kiss your royal feet.

KING OF CASTILE: Let him come in, and go notify Don Juan that he need wait no longer.

[*Enter* BATRICIO *and* GACENO.]

BATRICIO: My lord, why are such enormities allowed? Your own servants outrage the poor people of the land.

KING OF CASTILE: What are you saying?

BATRICIO: Don Juan Tenorio, detestable traitor that he is, stole my wife from me the night of my marriage, before its consummation. I have brought witnesses with me.

[*Enter* TISBEA *and* ISABELA.]

TISBEA: If Your Highness does not bring Don Juan to justice, I will complain to God and to men as long as I live. The sea cast him adrift; I gave him life and hospitality; and to reward my kindness he lied to me with the name of husband.

KING OF CASTILE: What are you saying?

ISABELA: She is telling the truth.

[*Enter* ARMINTA *and* OCTAVIO.]

ARMINTA: Where is my husband?

KING OF CASTILE: Whom do you mean?

ARMINTA: Don't you know? My husband is Don Juan Tenorio. I am here to be married to him. So he swore to me. He is a nobleman and cannot forswear. My lord, give orders for my wedding.

[*Enter* MARQUIS DE LA MOTA.]

MARQUIS: It is time, my lord, to bring the truth to light. Know that Don Juan Tenorio is guilty of the crime imputed to me. Though he was my friend, he brutally deceived me. I have two witnesses to bear me out.

KING OF CASTILE: Is this shamelessness possible? Don Juan must be arrested and executed.

DON DIEGO: Yes, let him be arrested and punished. I ask it as a reward for my services to the crown, lest heaven punish me for the wickedness of my son.

KING OF CASTILE: This is how my favorites behave!

[*Enter* CATALINÓN.]

CATALINÓN: Gentlemen, listen to the strangest event the world has ever witnessed. Listen! and kill me afterward if you wish. Don Juan was mocking the statue of the Commander the day before yesterday. To insult the dead man, he pulled the Statue's beard and invited him to supper. Fool that he was! The Statue came, and returned the invitation. We went to the church, and there, when supper was over, after a thousand horrible signs, the Statue grasped his hand and squeezed it till he died, and said, "God commands me to kill you thus in punishment for your crimes. As a man sows, so shall he reap."

KING OF CASTILE: What are you saying?

CATALINÓN: It's the truth. And before he died, my master cried out that he had not touched Doña Ana's honor, because she recognized him in time.

MARQUIS: I could kiss you for this news!

KING OF CASTILE: Heaven is just! Now then, Don Juan is dead; there is no impediment to a marriage between Isabela and Duke Octavio.

OCTAVIO: I receive her with gratitude, my lord, now that she is a widow.

MARQUIS: And I shall marry my cousin.

BATRICIO: And we'll marry our own girls in order to bring the true story of the guest of stone to an end.

KING OF CASTILE: And let the tomb be carried to the church of St. Francis in Madrid where it will be revered as it deserves.

MOLIÈRE

Don John; or, The Libertine

A Comedy

(1665)

Translated by John Ozell,
revised and augmented by Oscar Mandel

EDITOR'S NOTE

John Ozell's English version of *Dom Juan, ou Le Festin de Pierre* was first printed in 1714. Without having anything like the genius of Dryden to bring to his translations, Ozell had one resource denied even to the best modern translator (and who has done Molière justice?)—namely the English language of 1700, not only most suitable for Molière, but strong, flexible, pure, and elegant in itself. I did not hesitate to prefer his version to any of those which have followed, even though Ozell knew only the mutilated text. In the present text the gaps are filled with as little trace of repair work as possible, and a number of lapses are, I hope, corrected. Where eighteenth-century printing style might inconvenience the reader I have modernized Ozell's text, but chiefly with respect to punctuation, paragraphing, and to such typographical features as italicized proper names and place names. For the most part the original spelling has been retained, and in other details the text follows the 1714 edition.

TEXTS

The Works of Monsieur Molière, vol. VI. London: Lintot, 1714.
Molière, *Oeuvres*, vol. V. Edited by Despois and Mesnard. Paris: 1912.

DRAMATIS PERSONAE

Men

Don Louis, *Father to Don John*
Don John, *his Son*
Don Carlos, ⎱
Don Alonso, ⎰ *Brothers to Elvira*
The Statue of the Governor
Francisco, *a poor Man*
Mr. Sunday, *a Tradesman*
Sganarelle, *Servant to Don John*
Pierrot, *a Countryman*
Gusman, *Usher to Elvira*
Violette, ⎱
Ragotin, ⎰ *Lacquies to Don John*
Ramee, *a Hector*
A Pauper*
Don John's Followers
Don Carlos' and Don Alonso's Followers
A Ghost

Women

Donna Elvira, *Wife to Don John*
Charlotta, ⎱
Mathurina, ⎰ *Countrywomen*

Scene *lyes in Sicily*.

*This character did not appear in the version followed by Ozell. [*Editor's note*.]

ACT I

Scene 1

Sganarelle, Gusman

SGANARELLE [*with a Tobacco-Box in his Hand*]: Let Aristotle and all the Philosophers in the World say what they will, nothing is like Tobacco; 'tis the Darling of all Men of Honour, and he that lives without Tobacco is not worthy of Life. It not only gladdens and purges Man's Brain, but it likewise puts him in the way to Virtue, and one learns with it to become an honest Man. Don't you see that as soon as ever one takes it, with what an obliging Manner one uses everybody, and how glad one is to give it on all sides, be one where he will? We don't so much as stay till 'tis ask'd for, but prevent People's wishes; so true it is that Tobacco inspires all those that take it with Sentiments of Generosity and Virtue. But enough of this; let's resume the Thread of our Discourse. So your Mistress, dear Gusman, Donna Elvira, surprised at our Departure, set out after us; and her Heart, which my Master has pierced too deeply, cannot live, you say, without coming hither to him? Shall I give you my Opinion? I'm afraid that she'll be but ill rewarded for her Love; and that her Journey to this City will produce but little Fruit. You'd as good ha' stay'd at home.

GUSMAN: And pray, Sganarelle, tell me, what can inspire you with such an ill Augury? Has your Master open'd his Heart to you upon that Subject, and has he told you that some Coldness for her made him leave us?

SGANARELLE: No; but by what I see I can guess how things are, and tho' he has not yet told me anything, I could lay a Wager that there the Shoe pinches. Perhaps I may be deceived, but yet in such cases Experience has given me some knowledge.

GUSMAN: What! Could this sudden Departure proceed from Don John's Infidelity? Could he so far abuse Elvira's chaste Flame?

SGANARELLE: No, but he is young and fears—

GUSMAN: Could a Man of his Quality do so base an Action?

SGANARELLE: His Quality! A fine Reason truly! Why 'tis not that will prevent him.

GUSMAN: But the sacred Tyes of Marriage engage him.

SGANARELLE: Ah! Friend Gusman, you're but little acquainted with Don John, I see.

GUSMAN: 'Tis true, I am not, if he be so perfidious to us; and I can't imagine how after so much Love and Impatience, so many pressing Homages, Vows, Sighs, Tears, so many passionate Letters, burning Protestations, reiterated Oaths; so many Transports, and so much Warmth as he testify'd, even to force the sacred Obstacle of a Nunnery to put Donna Elvira in his Power; I say, I can't imagine how, after all this, he can have the Heart to break his Word.

SGANARELLE: I don't find it so difficult to imagine; and if you knew the Spark thoroughly, you'd think it no such hard thing. I don't say he has changed his Sentiments for Donna Elvira, I am not yet sure on't. You know I set out before him by his Order, and since his Arrival he has not yet talk'd to me, but by way of forewarning I must tell you (under the Rose) that you behold in my Master, Don John, the greatest Libertine that the Earth ever bore, a Madman, a Dog, a Devil, a Turk, an Heretick, that believes neither Heaven nor Hell, nor Devil; who lives like a downright Brute-Beast, one of Epicurus' Swine, a true Sardanapalus, that stops his Ears to every Christian Remonstrance that can be made to him, and esteems all we believe as idle Trash. You tell me he has marry'd your Mistress; he'd ha' done more to ha' satisfy'd his Passion, and besides her would have marry'd you, her Cat, and her Dog. A Marriage don't cost him much, it is his accustom'd Snare to entrap the fair Sex; and he's a Marryer at all Adventures; Damsel, Gentlewoman, Citizen's Wife, Country-lass, nothing's too hot or too cold for him; and if I were to tell you the Names of all those he has marry'd in several Places, 'twould be a Chapter that would last till Night.

You are surprised and change Colour at what I tell you; yet this is only a Sketch of him; and there's need of other strokes of the Pencil to finish his Picture. 'Tis enough to tell you that Heav'n must needs overwhelm him some Day or other, that I had better belong to the Devil than to him, and that he makes me Witness of so many Horrors that I could wish he were I know not where. But a wicked Lord is a terrible thing; I must be faithful to him in spite of my Teeth*; Fear performs in me the Duty of Zeal, bridles my Thoughts, and often obliges me to applaud what in my Heart I detest.

Here, he's coming to walk in the Palace; let's part. I have told you

---

*In spite of myself. [*Editor's note.*]

all this freely, and it came a little hastily out o' my Mouth; but if ever any on't comes to his Hearing, I'll promise you I shall be so free as to tell you you lye in your Throat.

Scene 2

Don John, Sganarelle

DON JOHN: What Man was that? He look'd like Donna Elvira's Gusman.

SGANARELLE: Something like him, indeed.

DON JOHN: What! Was't he?

SGANARELLE: He himself.

DON JOHN: How long has he been in this City?

SGANARELLE: Ever since yesterday Evening.

DON JOHN: What brings him hither?

SGANARELLE: I believe you may guess what disturbs him.

DON JOHN: Our Departure, I suppose.

SGANARELLE: The good Man is sadly mortify'd with it, and ask'd me the Cause of't.

DON JOHN: And what Answer did you give?

SGANARELLE: I said you had not told me anything about it.

DON JOHN: But what do you think of it? What do you imagine about this Affair?

SGANARELLE: Why, I believe, without wronging you, there's some new Love in the Case.

DON JOHN: You believe it?

SGANARELLE: Yes.

DON JOHN: Faith, you're not deceiv'd; I must confess another Object has driven Elvira out of my Head.

SGANARELLE: O, Don John, I know at my Finger's Ends that your Heart is the greatest Wanderer in the World; it loves to ramble from Bonds to Bonds, and hates to stay long in a Place.

DON JOHN: And, tell me, do you not think I am in the right to do what I do?

SGANARELLE: Ha, Sir!

DON JOHN: Speak.

SGANARELLE: Yes, to be sure you're in the right. If you have a Mind to it, nobody can contradict it. But if you have not a Mind to't, it may be the Case is alter'd.

DON JOHN: Well, I give you leave to speak, and to tell me your Thoughts.

SGANARELLE: Why then, Sir, I must freely tell you I don't approve of your Method, and I think it a very ill thing to make Court to everybody, as you do.

DON JOHN: What! Wou'd you have me stick to the first Object that takes me, to renounce the World for that, and have no more Eyes for anybody? A fine thing indeed to pique oneself on a false Honour of being faithful, to bury oneself for ever in one Passion, and to be dead from one's very Youth to all other Beauties that may strike our Eyes. No, no, Constancy is fit for none but Fools, all the Fair Sex have a right to Charm us, and the Advantage of being first met with ought not to deprive the others of the just Pretensions they all have upon our Hearts. For my part, Beauty ravishes me wherever I meet with it; and I easily give way to the sweet Violence with which it hurries us along. Though I am engaged, my Love for one Belle does not engage me to do Injustice to all the rest; I have Eyes for the Merit of all, and render to every one the Homage and Tribute to which we're oblig'd by Nature. However it be, I can't refuse my Heart to any that I think amiable, and when a handsome Face demands it of me, if I had Ten Thousand I shou'd give 'em all. Rising Inclinations, after all, have inexpressible Charms, and all the Pleasure of Love lies in Variety. One tastes an extreme delight in reducing by an hundred Contrivances the Heart of a young Beauty; to see the Progress we daily make in it; to combat by Transports, Sighs, and Tears the innocent Virtue of a Soul, which can hardly prevail with itself to yield; to demolish Inch by Inch all the little Resistances that oppose us; to vanquish the Scruples on which she prides herself, and to lead her gently whither we would have her go. But when one is once Master there is nothing further to be said nor wish'd for; all the Charms of the Passion are over, and we sleep in the Tranquility of such a Love unless some new Object come to awaken our Desires and present to our Heart the attracting Charms of another Conquest to undertake. In short, nothing is so sweet as to triumph over the Resistance of a beautiful Person; and in that I have the Ambition of Conquerors, who fly perpetually from Victory to Victory and can never prevail with themselves to put a bound to their Wishes. Nothing can restrain the Impetuosity of my Desires; I have an Heart for the whole Earth; and like Alexander, I cou'd wish for new Worlds wherein to extend my Amorous Conquests.

SGANARELLE: Body o' me, how you talk! One wou'd think you had learn't this by Heart; you speak like a Book.

DON JOHN: What have you to say to't!

SGANARELLE: Faith, I have to say—I don't know what I have to say; for you turn things in such a Manner that one wou'd believe you are right, and yet you are not. I had the finest Thoughts in the World, and your Discourse has put 'em all out o' my Head, but another time I'll write down my Arguments to dispute with you.

DON JOHN: Do so.

SGANARELLE: But, Sir, wou'd it be included in the Permission you have given me if I told you that I am a trifle scandaliz'd with the Life you lead?

DON JOHN: How! What Life do I lead?

SGANARELLE: A very good one. But to marry every Month as you do—

DON JOHN: Can there be anything more agreeable?

SGANARELLE: 'Tis true, I believe it may be very agreeable and very diverting; I myself cou'd swallow it if there were no harm in't. But, Sir, to make a Jest of a holy Sacrament, which—

DON JOHN: Come, come, 'tis a Question between Heaven and me, which we'll resolve without troubling your Head.

SGANARELLE: Faith, Sir, I've heard it said 'tis but a scurvy Jest to Jest with Heaven, and that Libertines never come to a good End.

DON JOHN: Have not I told you, Mr. Fool, that I did not love Remonstrances?

SGANARELLE: God forbid I shou'd say this to you, you best know what you have to do; and if you believe nothing, you have your Reasons for't; but there are some little impertinent People in the World who are unbelievers without knowing why, who pretend to be Freethinkers because they imagine it fits well upon 'em, and if I had such a Master I wou'd plainly say to him, looking in his Face: Are you bold enough to mock Heaven? Do you not tremble to scoff as you do against the most sacred things? It agrees mighty well for you indeed, little Worm, little Shrimp (I speak to the Master I mention'd), it agrees mighty well with you indeed to turn into Jest what other Men revere. Do you think that because you're a Man of Quality, have a fair well-curl'd Wig, a Feather in your Hat, a laced Suit of Cloaths and flame-colour'd Ribbans (I don't speak to you but to t'other), do you think, quo' I, that you're e'er the wiser, that everything's lawful for you to do, and that you are not to be put in your place? Know from me that am your Servant that Heaven sooner or later punishes the Impious, that a wicked Life leads to a wicked Death, that—

DON JOHN: Peace.

SGANARELLE: Why, what's to be done?

DON JOHN: I must tell you that a Beauty sticks in my Heart, and that attracted by her Charms I have follow'd her quite to this City.

SGANARELLE: And Sir, have you no Terror upon your Spirits for the Death of the Governor you kill'd here Six Months ago?

DON JOHN: Why Terror? Did not I kill him well?

SGANARELLE: Very well, extraordinary well; he has no Cause to complain on't.

DON JOHN: I have had my Pardon for this Affair.

SGANARELLE: Ay, but perhaps this Pardon don't extinguish the Resentment of Relations and Friends, and—

DON JOHN: Oh, don't let's think of the harm that may happen to us, but only of what may give us Pleasure. The Person I speak of is a young Gentlewoman (the most agreeable in the World) newly betroth'd, and brought hither by the Man that's to marry her. Chance shew'd me these two Lovers three or four Days before their Voyage. Never did I see two Persons so satisfy'd with one another, and shew so much Love. The visible Tenderness of their mutual Ardour disturb'd me; it struck me to the Heart, and my Love began by Jealousy. Yes, I cou'd not bear to see 'em so content together, Indignation allarm'd my Desires, and I thought it wou'd be an extreme Pleasure to spoil their Accord and break that Affection, the Delicacy whereof offended my Heart. But hitherto all my Endeavours have been in vain, and I now have recourse to the last Remedy. The intended Husband is today to take the air with his Mistress on the Sea. I have, without letting you know anything of the matter, already prepared everything to satisfy my Love, and I have a little Bark and Men ready, with whom I may very easily run away with the Fair One.

SGANARELLE: Ha! Sir—

DON JOHN: What!

SGANARELLE: You do very well; there's nothing like contenting oneself.

DON JOHN: Then be ready to go along with me, and take care to get all my Arms, that—[*He perceives Donna Elvira.*] O unhappy meeting! Traitor, you did not tell me that she herself was here.

SGANARELLE: Sir, you did not ask me.

DON JOHN: Sure she is mad not to change her Dress, but to come hither in her country Suit.

Scene 3

Donna Elvira, Don John, Sganarelle

DONNA ELVIRA: Will you do me the Favour, Don John, to recognize me? May I at least hope you'll turn your Face this way?

DON JOHN: Madam, I must confess I am surprised, and did not expect you here.

DONNA ELVIRA: Yes, I see you did not expect me, and you are indeed surpriz'd, but quite otherwise than I hoped for; and the manner of your Surprise fully satisfies me in what I before refused to believe. I marvel at my Simplicity and the Weakness of my Heart to doubt a Treason which so many Appearances confirm'd me in. I confess I was very good, or rather very foolish, to try to deceive myself and contradict my Eyes and Judgment. I search'd for Reasons to excuse to my Tenderness the Remissness of Friendship it perceived in you, and I forged an hundred lawful Causes for so hasty a Departure, to justify you from the Crime which my Reason accused you of. In vain my just Suspicion daily advised me. I rejected its Voice, which represented you as criminal, and I listen'd with Pleasure to an hundred ridiculous Chimeras which described you innocent to my Heart. But now this Reception gives no further room for Doubt, and the Look you receiv'd me with teaches me many more things than I wou'd willingly know. Yet I shou'd be very glad to hear from your own Mouth the Cause of your Departure. Pray speak, Don John, and let me see with what Air you are able to justifie yourself.

DON JOHN: Madam, there's Sganarelle can tell you why I came away.

SGANARELLE: I, Sir? By your leave, I know nothing of the Matter.

DONNA ELVIRA: Well then, Sganarelle, speak; it don't signify from whose Mouth I hear his Reasons.

DON JOHN [*making Signs to Sganarelle to go nearer*]: Come, speak to the Lady.

SGANARELLE: What wou'd you have me say to her?

DONNA ELVIRA: Come nearer, since he'll have it so, and tell me the Cause of so sudden a Journey.

DON JOHN: Why don't you answer?

SGANARELLE: I have nothing to answer; you are pleas'd to be merry with your Servant.

DON JOHN: Will you answer, I say?

SGANARELLE: Madam—

DONNA ELVIRA: What?

SGANARELLE [*turning to his Master*]: Sir—

DON JOHN [*threatening him*]: If—

SGANARELLE: Madam, the Conquerors, Alexander, and the new Worlds caused our Departure. This is all I can say, Sir.

DONNA ELVIRA: Pray do you, Don John, explain these fine Mysteries.

DON JOHN: Madam, to tell you the Truth—

DONNA ELVIRA: You a Courtier, accustom'd to these things, and defend yourself no better? I pity you to see you in this Confusion; why don't you arm yourself with a noble Impudence? Why don't you swear that you have still the same Sentiments for me, that you still love me with an unparallel'd Ardour, and that nothing can unbind you from me but Death? Why don't you tell me that Affairs of the utmost Consequence obliged you to depart without my Knowledge? That in spite of your Teeth you must remain here for some time, and that I may return from whence I came, assur'd that you'll follow my steps as soon as may be? That you burn to be at home, and that being absent from me you endure the Pains of a Body separated from its Soul? Thus you ought to defend yourself, and not be so Thunderstruck.

DON JOHN: I must confess, Madam, I have not the Talent of Dissimulation, and wear a sincere Heart. I won't tell you that I've still the same Sentiments for you, and that I burn to be with you, since 'tis certain I came away only to avoid you; not for the Reasons you imagine, but out of a pure Motive of Conscience, and because I did not think I could live with you any longer but in Sin. Scruples took me, Madam, and I open'd the Eyes of my Soul to what I was doing. I reflected that to marry you I had forced the Gate of a Convent, that you broke the Vows which engaged you elsewhere, and that Heav'n is very jealous of such Things. Repentance seiz'd me, and I fear'd the Wrath of Heav'n. I thought our Marriage was but a disguis'd Adultery, that it would bring some disgrace from above upon us, and that I ought to endeavour to forget you, and give you an Opportunity of returning to your former Obligations. Wou'd you oppose so holy a Design, Madam? I'd have Heaven upon my hands by keeping you; and—

DONNA ELVIRA: O impious Wretch, 'tis now that I know you thoroughly; and to my Misfortune I know you too late. Such a Knowledge can only serve to make me run mad. But your Crime shall not long remain unpunish'd; and the same Heav'n you mock will revenge me of your Perfidiousness.

DON JOHN: Heaven, Sganarelle!

SGANARELLE: Forsooth! We care not a straw for that, we two.

DON JOHN: Madam—

DONNA ELVIRA: 'Tis enough, I'll hear no more, and I am sorry I have heard so much. 'Tis a Meanness to hear one's Shame express'd too plain; and in such Cases a noble Heart should take its Resolution at the first Word. Don't expect that I'll break out into Reproaches and Abuses; no, no, my Wrath is not one that will exhale in vain Words; all its Heat is reserved for Revenge. I tell you again, Heav'n will punish you, perfidious Wretch, for this Deed; and if Heav'n has nothing in it that terrifies you, be at least afraid of an offended Woman.

SGANARELLE: If he should be touch'd with Remorse now!

DON JOHN [*after a little Consideration*]: Come, let's about our amorous Enterprize.

SGANARELLE: O what an abominable Master am I obliged to serve!

ACT II

Scene 1

Charlotta, Pierrot

CHARLOTTA: 'S Bodykins, Pierrot, yau ceame thither just i' th' nick.

PIERROT: Marry, they weare within eames eace of being drawn'd, boath of 'um.

CHARLOTTA: What, the high Wind that was i' th' Morning overturn'd 'um into th' Sea?

PIERROT: I'll tell it yau all, just as't fell out; for, as the saying is, I first spy'd 'um, 'twas mea that first spy'd 'um. I and fat Lucas was on the Sea shoar, and was amusing ourselves with throwing Clods of Yearth at one another's Heads; for you know, fat Lucas loves to be pleaying, and sometaimes I pleay too. Therefore as we were pleaying, for pleaying we was, I spy'd a huge weay off something that stirr'd in the Weater, and which ceame towards us, shake, shake. I look'd steadfastly on't, and all of a sudden I saw that I saw nought any longer. O Lucas, says I, I think I see two Men swimming dawn thear. Marry, says he, your Sight's dimm. 'Sdeath, says I, my Sight ben't dimm, they're Men. Not at all, say's he, you are purblind. Will you lay a Weager, says I, that I ben't purblind, says I, and that they be two Men, says I, that are swimming this weay, says I? 'Znigs, says he, I lay a Weager, no! Will you lay ten Pence, says I. With all my Heart, says he; and to sheaw yau, there's the Mony dawn, says he. I was neither Fool nor Dunce, I breavely throaws dawn four Pieces with Marks, and five Pence in Doubles; by th' Mass, as boldly as if I had drank oaff a Gleass of Wine; for I am ventersom and dash at a Venture. Yet I kneaw what I dud, to be sure. I had scant leay'd, but I saw the two Men pleain, who made a sign to us to goa fetch 'um, and I teakes up the Steakes. Come, Lucas, says I, you see theay call us; come quickly and help 'um. Noa, says he, they ha' made me lose. To cut shoart my Tale, I rattled soa that wea got into a Boat, and then we meade such ado that we got 'um out o' th' Weater, and then I carry'd 'um hoame to our House, before the Fire, and then they pull'd oaff all their Cloaths to dry 'umselves, and then two moare of the seame Gang ceame, who seaved 'umselves, and then Mathurina ceame, and he ogled her. This is all that was done, Charlotta.

CHARLOTTA: Did not yau tell me, Pierrot, that one of 'um is handsomer than the rest?

PIERROT: Yea, that's the Master; he is some great great Gentleman to be sure, for he has Gold upon his Cloaths from top to bottom, and those that serve'n are Gentlefolk themselves; and yet, as great a Mon as he is, by th' Mass, he'd been drawn'd if I had not come as I dud.

CHARLOTTA: Good lack!

PIERROT: 'Twas certainly so.

CHARLOTTA: Is he still naked at your House, Pierrot?

PIERROT: No, they dress'd 'umselves before us. Lord, I never beheld People dress themselves so in my born; the whim whams thoase Courtiers put on! I shou'd be confounded to do't, for my part, and I was ameaz'd to see't. Why, Charlotta, they had Heare which didn't grow to their Heads, and they put it on like a Cap. They have Shirts which have Sleeves as you and I might easily get into. Instead of Breeches, they wear a Wardrobe as big as from hence to Easter; instead of Doublets, they wear little tiny Wastecoats that doant reach dawn to their Arse; and instead of Cravats, great Neck-Handkerchiefs with four huge Tufts of Linnen which hang dawn o' their Breasts. They ha' other little Cravats too about their Arms, and great swathes o' lace at their Legs; and among all this, soa many Ribbans, soa many Ribbans, that 'tis a downraight pity. The very Shoas are stuff'd with 'um from one end to t'other, and they are meade in such a foarm that I shud break my Neck with 'um.

CHARLOTTA: Faith, Pierrot, I mun go sea this.

PIERROT: O steay a little, Charlotta, I ha' something to say t'ye.

CHARLOTTA: Well, what is't?

PIERROT: Do you see, Charlotta, as the saying is, I mun leay open my Heart to yau. I love ye, you know it, and we are to be marry'd; but by th' Mass, I e'nt satisfy'd with ye.

CHARLOTTA: Why, what's the matter?

PIERROT: The Matter is that you make me plaguy mad.

CHARLOTTA: How!

PIERROT: By th' Mass, you don't love me.

CHARLOTTA: O, is that all?

PIERROT: Yea, that's all, and enough too.

CHARLOTTA: Law, Pierrot, yau always tell ma the seame thing.

PIERROT: I always tell yau the seame thing, because 'tis always the seame thing; and if it was not always the seame thing, I shud not always tell yau the seame thing.

CHARLOTTA: But what wou'd you have?

PIERROT: Marry, I'd ha' yau love me.

CHARLOTTA: Why? Doa'nt I?

PIERROT: Noa, you doan't love me, and yet I do all I con to meake yau. I buy you—no offence—Ribbans of all the Men that go by, I go venture my Neck o' th' Rocks to get you Shells, I make those that play upon the Cymbal play for you when 'tis your Birthday, and I might as well run my Head against the Wall. Do you see, 'tis not honest not to love thoase that love us.

CHARLOTTA: Why I do love you.

PIERROT: Aye, mightily indeed!

CHARLOTTA: How wou'd you ha' ma do?

PIERROT: I'd ha' yau do as People do when they love as they ought.

CHARLOTTA: Why, don't I love yau as I ought?

PIERROT: No; People play an hundred little Tricks when they love heartily. Do you see fat Thomassa, how fond she is of young Robin? She's always about him to provoke'n, and never lets'n be at quiet. She's always putting some Trick or other upon him, or always cuffing him as she goes by; and t'other Day as he was sitting on a Joint-Stool, she pull'd it from under'n, and made him fall all along. See how People do when they love; but you ne'er speake a Word to ma, yau always stand like a Block, and I may goa by yau twenty times and you never gi' me the least Blow, nor speak the least Word to me. By th' Mass, this is not feair, you're too caud.

CHARLOTTA: What wou'd yau ha' ma do? I can't alter myself.

PIERROT: Yes yau can. When one loves anybody, one always give some Token or other that a Body loves.

CHARLOTTA: I love yau as much as I can; and if that doan't satisfie you, you may love somebody else an you will.

PIERROT: I say'd so. If you lov'd ma, wou'd you talk thus?

CHARLOTTA: Why do you come to plague a body then?

PIERROT: Why, what harm do I do you? I only desire a little Friendship from you.

CHARLOTTA: Well, let me alone and don't be so heasty; perhaps it may come all of a sudden, when we think nothing o' th' matter.

PIERROT: Shake Hands then, Charlotta.

CHARLOTTA: Well, there.

PIERROT: Promise me, then, to try to love ma more.

CHARLOTTA: I'll do all I con, but it must come of itself. Pierrot, is that the Gentleman?

PIERROT: Yea, that's he.

CHARLOTTA: Lord, how pretty he is! What a pity it wou'd ha' been if he had been drawn'd.

PIERROT: I'll be back presently; I'll go teake a Pint to refresh myself for the trouble I've had.

Scene 2

Don John, Sganarelle, Charlotta

DON JOHN: We have miss'd our Aim, Sganarelle, and that sudden Storm has, together with our Bark, o'erthrown the Project we had form'd. But to tell you the truth, the Countrywoman I just now left makes amends for this Misfortune, and I have observed in her Charms which efface from my Mind all the Spleen that the ill Success of our Enterprise gave me. That Heart must not escape me, and I have already so dispos'd it that it won't need many Sighs.

SGANARELLE: Sir, I must confess it, you amaze me; we're scarce escap'd from the danger of Death when, instead of thanking Heaven for the Pity it was pleased to take on us, you labour anew to incur its Anger by your old Fancies; and your Amours incr—peace, Knave, you don't know what you say; your Master best knows what he has to do. Come.

DON JOHN [*perceiving Charlotta*]: Whence comes this other Lass? Sganarelle, did you ever see anything prettier? Tell me, don't you think this as good as t'other?

SGANARELLE: Certainly. [*Aside.*] Another Piece!

DON JOHN: Well met, pretty Lass! What! Are there such handsome Creatures as you amongst these Fields, these Trees, and Rocks?

CHARLOTTA: I am as you see, Sir.

DON JOHN: Are you of this Village?

CHARLOTTA: Yes, Sir.

DON JOHN: And live here?

CHARLOTTA: Yes, Sir.

DON JOHN: What's your Name?

CHARLOTTA: Charlotta, Sir, at your Service.

DON JOHN: Ah what a fine Person 'tis! What piercing Eyes!

CHARLOTTA: Sir, you make me ashamed.

DON JOHN: O don't be ashamed at the Truth. Sganarelle, what do you say to her? Can anything be more agreeable? Pray turn a little; what a fine Shape! Hold up your Head a little; and what a pretty Face! Open your Eyes quite; O how fine they are! Pray let me see your Teeth; how amorous they are; and those provoking Lips. For my part I am ravish'd, and never beheld so charming a Person.

CHARLOTTA: Sir, you are pleas'd to say all this; I can't tell whether you make a Jest of me or no.

DON JOHN: I make a Jest of you! God forbid! I love you too well for that; I speak from the bottom of my Heart.

CHARLOTTA: If it be so, I'm oblig'd to you.

DON JOHN: Not at all; you are not at all oblig'd to me for what I say; you owe it to your Beauty alone.

CHARLOTTA: Sir, these are too fine Words for me. I have not wit to answer you.

DON JOHN: Sganarelle, look on her Hands.

CHARLOTTA: Fie, Sir, they're as black as I don't know what.

DON JOHN: Ha! What say you; they are the finest in the World; pray let me kiss 'em.

CHARLOTTA: Sir, you do me too much Honour; if I had dreamt of this, I would not ha' fail'd to ha' wash'd 'em with Bran.

DON JOHN: Pretty Charlotta, you are not marry'd, are you?

CHARLOTTA: No, Sir, but I am soon to be, with Pierrot, Son to Goody Simonetta.

DON JOHN: What! Shou'd such a one as you be Wife to a Peasant! No, no; that's a Profanation of so much Beauty. You was not born to live in a Village. You certainly deserve a better Fortune, and Heaven,

which knows it well, brought me hither on purpose to hinder this
Marriage and do justice to your Charms; for in short, fair Charlotta,
I love you with all my Heart, and if you'll consent I'll deliver you
from this miserable Place, and put you in the Condition you deserve.
This Love is doubtless sudden, but 'tis an Effect of your great Beauty.
I love You as much in a quarter of an Hour as I shou'd another in
six Months.

CHARLOTTA: Truly, Sir, I don't know what to do when you speak. Your
Words make me glad, and I shou'd be mighty desirous to believe
you; but I was always told that one shou'd never believe Gentlemen,
and that you Courtiers are Sharpers, who think of nothing but
abusing Maidens.

DON JOHN: I am none of those sort of People.

SGANARELLE: [Aside.] No, to be sure!

CHARLOTTA: Do you see, Sir, there's no Pleasure in suffering oneself to
be abused. I am a poor Countrywoman, but I value my Reputation,
and had rather be dead than dishonour'd.

DON JOHN: What! Do you think me so wicked as to abuse such a one
as you, and so base as to dishonour you! No, no: I have too much
Conscience to do any such thing. I love you, Charlotta, virtuously
and honourably, and to shew you that I speak the Truth, know that
I have no other Design than to marry you. Wou'd you desire a
greater Testimony of it? I am ready to do it when you will, and I
take that Man to be witness of the Promise I make you.

SGANARELLE: Never fear; he'll marry you as much as you will.

DON JOHN: Ah, Charlotta! I plainly perceive you are not yet acquainted with me. You do me wrong to Judge of me by others, and
if there are Cheats in the World, Men who think of nothing but
abusing Maidens, you ought to scratch me out of the Number, and
not to question my Sincerity. Besides, your Beauty may be a sufficient
Assurance to you. When a Woman's made like you, she need never
have such Fears. Believe me, you have not the Air of one that's to
be abus'd, and for my part, I confess, I'd pierce my Heart with a
thousand Wounds if I had the least Thought of betraying you.

CHARLOTTA: Lord, I can't tell whether what you say is true or no, but
you make a Body believe you.

DON JOHN: When you believe me, you'll certainly do me Justice, and
I again repeat the Promise I have made. Do you accept it? Won't you
consent to be my Wife?

CHARLOTTA: Yes, if my Aunt will.

DON JOHN: Give me your Hand then, Charlotta, since I have your Consent.

CHARLOTTA: But pray, Sir, don't deceive me now; 'twou'd be a Sin; and you see I do what I do Innocently.

DON JOHN: What, do you still doubt my Sincerity? Will you ha' me swear frightful Oaths? May Heav'n—

CHARLOTTA: Lord, don't swear; I believe you.

DON JOHN: Give me a little Kiss then, in earnest of your Word.

CHARLOTTA: Oh, Sir, stay 'till I be marry'd; then I'll kiss you as much as you will.

DON JOHN: Well, Charlotta, I'll do whatever you please; only give me your Hand, and let me by a thousand Kisses express the Rapture I am—

Scene 3

Don John, Sganarelle, Pierrot, Charlotta

PIERROT [getting between 'em, and pushing away Don John]: Soft and fair, Sir, if you please; you heat yourself too much; you may hap' get a Purisie.

DON JOHN [pushing away Pierrot roughly]: Who sent for this Impertinent?

PIERROT: Be at quiet, and don't be caressing our Brides.

DON JOHN [continuing to thrust him away]: The noisy Fellow!

PIERROT: S'heart, People aren't to be push'd thus.

CHARLOTTA [taking Pierrot by the Arm]: Let him alone, Pierrot.

PIERROT: How do you mean, let'n alone? I woan't, not I.

DON JOHN: What!

PIERROT: 'Znigs, because you're a Gentleman, you come to tickle our Wives under our Noses; go and tickle your own.

DON JOHN: Hey day!

PIERROT: Ay, and hey day too! [DON JOHN gives him Box on the Ear.] 'Sbodykins, don't strike me. [Another.] 'Sdeath. [Another.] 'Zblood. [Another.] 'Sheart, 'tis not Fair to beat Folk thus. Is this my Reward for saving you from being drawn'd?

CHARLOTTA: Pierrot, don't be angry.

PIERROT: I will be angry; and you're a Hussy to let yourself be cuddled.

CHARLOTTA: O Pierrot, there's more in the cease than you think for; the Gentleman will marry me, and you ought not to put yourself into a Passion.

PIERROT: Aye! When you're engaged to me?

CHARLOTTA: That's nothing, Pierrot; if you love me, shou'd not you be glad to see me a Gentlewoman?

PIERROT: No; I'd rather see you hang'd than another's.

CHARLOTTA: Go, go, Pierrot, don't trouble yourself; if I am a Gentlewoman you shall get something by 't, and you shall serve us with Butter and Cheese.

PIERROT: S'death, I won't, tho' you peay'd me double for't. Do you hearken thus to what he says? 'Sheart, if I had Thought of this before, he might ha' drawn'd for me; I'd ha' given 'n a Blow on his Head with my Oar.

DON JOHN [*coming up to Pierrot to strike him*]: What's that you say?

PIERROT [*getting behind Charlotta*]: I fear no a Man.

DON JOHN [*going to him*]: Let me lay Hands on you—

PIERROT [*gets on t'other side Charlotta*]: I doan't ceare, not I.

DON JOHN [*running after him*]: We'll try that.

PIERROT [*escapes behind Charlotta again*]: I ha' seen Gentlefolk before now.

DON JOHN: Ha' ye.

SGANARELLE: Lord Sir, let the poor Fellow alone. 'Tis a pity to beat him. Go, honest Man, and don't speak to him.

PIERROT [*gets by Sganarelle and speaks boldly to Don John*]: I will speak to 'en.

DON JOHN [*Lifts up his Hand to give Pierrot a Blow, who Pops down his Head, and Sganarelle receives the Blow.*]: I'll teach you to—

SGANARELLE [*looking upon Pierrot, who stoop'd to avoid the Blow*]: Plague take the Booby!

DON JOHN: You're rewarded for your Charity.

PIERROT: Faith, I'll go tell her Aunt all this.

DON JOHN: In short, I shall be the happiest of Mankind, and I wou'd not change my Fortune for all the things in the World. What Pleasure shall I have when you're my Wife! and—

Scene 4

Don John, Sganarelle, Charlotta, Mathurina

SGANARELLE [*perceiving Mathurina*]: Ah ha!

MATHURINA [*to Don John*]: Sir, what are you doing with Charlotta there? Are you talking to Her of Love too?

DON JOHN [*Aside to Mathurina.*]: No, on the contrary she testifies a desire to be my Wife, and I tell her I'm engag'd to you.

CHARLOTTA: What is't you want, Mathurina?

DON JOHN [*Aside to Charlotta.*]: She is jealous of my speaking to you and wou'd fain have me marry her, but I tell her 'tis you I would have.

MATHURINA: What! Charlotta—

DON JOHN [*Aside to Mathurina.*]: All you can say to her will be in vain. She has got that Fancy into her Head.

CHARLOTTA: What then, Mathurina—

DON JOHN [*Aside to Charlotta.*]: Your Words wou'd be in vain; you'd never get her off that Whim.

MATHURINA: Do you—

DON JOHN [*Aside to Mathurina.*]: She won't hear Reason.

CHARLOTTA: I'd—

DON JOHN [*Aside to Charlotta.*]: She's as Obstinate as the Devil.

MATHURINA: Truly—

DON JOHN [*Aside to Mathurina.*]: Say nothing to her; she's a mad Woman.

CHARLOTTA: I think—

DON JOHN [*Aside to Charlotta.*]: Let her alone; she's an extravagant Wretch.

MATHURINA: No, no, I must speak to her.

CHARLOTTA: I'll hear her Reasons.

MATHURINA: What—

DON JOHN [*Aside to Mathurina.*]: I'll lay you a Wager she tells you I promis'd to Marry her.

CHARLOTTA: I—

DON JOHN [*Aside to Charlotta.*]: I'll lay a Wager she affirms that I promised to take her for my Wife.

MATHURINA: 'Tis not well, Charlotta, to meddle with other Folks' Merchandise.

CHARLOTTA: 'Tis not fit, Mathurina, that you shou'd be Jealous because the Gentleman speaks to me.

MATHURINA: 'Twas me that the Gentleman first saw.

CHARLOTTA: If he saw you First, he saw me Second, and has promised to marry me.

DON JOHN [*Aside to Mathurina.*]: Well, did not I tell you so?

MATHURINA: I beg your Pardon, 'twas me and not you that he promised to Marry.

DON JOHN [*Aside to Charlotta.*]: Did not I guess this?

CHARLOTTA: You must tell that Tale to others; 'twas me he promised.

MATHURINA: Do you make a Jest of People? Once more, 'twas me.

CHARLOTTA: There he is; he'll tell you whether I'm in the right or no.

MATHURINA: There he is to contradict me if I tell a Lye.

CHARLOTTA: Sir, did you promise to marry her?

DON JOHN [*Aside to Charlotta.*]: You jest sure!

MATHURINA: Is it true, Sir, that you have given your Word to be her Husband?

DON JOHN [*Aside to Mathurina.*]: Cou'd you have such a Thought?

CHARLOTTA: You see she affirms it.

DON JOHN [*Aside to Charlotta.*]: Let her alone.

MATHURINA: You see how positive she is.

DON JOHN [*Aside to Mathurina.*]: Let her say what she will.

CHARLOTTA: No, no, we must know the Truth.

MATHURINA: We must have it decided.

CHARLOTTA: Yes, Mathurina, I'll ha' the Gentleman prove you a Noddy.

MATHURINA: Charlotta, I'll ha' the Gentleman prove you a Goose.

CHARLOTTA: Sir, pray decide the Quarrel.

MATHURINA: Satisfie us, Sir.

CHARLOTTA: You shall see.

MATHURINA: Ay, and you shall too.

CHARLOTTA [*to Don John*]: Speak.

MATHURINA [*to Don John*]: Speak.

DON JOHN [*being perplex'd, addresses himself to both*]: What wou'd you have me say? You both equally affirm that I promised to marry you. Does not each of you know the Truth without my explaining myself any farther? Why wou'd you oblige me to Repetitions? Has not she that I really promis'd wherewithal in herself to Laugh at what t'other says, and ought she to be disturb'd, provided I accomplish my Promise? Words are nothing, Deeds are all. Therefore by them only will I satisfie you, and when I marry, you shall see which of the two possesses my Heart. [*Aside to Mathurina.*] Let her believe what she will. [*Aside to Charlotta.*] Let her flatter herself in her Imagination. [*Aside to Mathurina.*] I adore you. [*Aside to Charlotta.*] I am entirely yours. [*Aside to Mathurina.*] All Faces are ugly in your Presence. [*Aside to Charlotta.*] One cannot bear others when one has seen you. I have some Commands to give; I'll return in a Quarter of an Hour.

CHARLOTTA [*to Mathurina*]: I am she he loves, however.

MATHURINA: 'Tis me he'll Marry.

SGANARELLE: Poor Girls! I pity your Innocence, and can't endure to see you run thus to your Destruction. Take my Advice, both of you: don't let his Stories fuddle you, and stay in your Village.

DON JOHN [*returning*]: I'd fain know why Sganarelle don't follow me.

SGANARELLE [*to the Girls*]: My Master is a Knave; his Design is only to abuse you, as he has several others; he is a Marryer of the whole Sex, and— [*Perceives Don John*] 'Tis false, and whosoever tells you so, you shou'd tell him he Lies. My Master is not the Marryer of the whole Sex; he's no Knave; he has no Design to abuse you, and never abused any others. O, there he is, ask him himself.

DON JOHN: Yes.

SGANARELLE: Sir, as the World is full of Backbiters, I was beforehand with 'em, and told 'em that if anybody shou'd tell 'em any Harm of you, that they shou'd not believe it but tell him he ly'd.

DON JOHN: Sganarelle.

SGANARELLE: Yes, my Master is a Man of Honour; I'll maintain it.

DON JOHN: Hemp!

SGANARELLE: They are Impertinents.

Scene 5

Don John, Ramee, Charlotta, Mathurina, Sganarelle

RAMEE: Sir, I come to inform you that you are not safe here.

DON JOHN: How so?

RAMEE: Twelve Men on Horseback are searching for you, and will be here in a Moment. I can't tell how they cou'd follow you, but I heard it of a Countryman whom they enquired of, and to whom they described you. The Affair presses, and the sooner you get from hence the better.

DON JOHN [*to Charlotta and Mathurina*]: An important Affair obliges me to be gone, but pray remember the Word I have given you, and believe you shall hear from me before tomorrow Night— [*Exeunt* MATHURINA *and* CHARLOTTA.] As the Match is unequal, I must use Stratagem, and the better to avoid the Misfortune that threatens me, Sganarelle shall dress in my Cloaths, and I—

SGANARELLE: A good Jest, to expose me to be kill'd in your Cloaths, and—

DON JOHN: Come quickly, I do you too much Honour, and happy is the Servant that can have the Glory of dying for his Master.

SGANARELLE: I thank you for your Glory. O Heav'ns, since Death is in the Case, grant me the Favour not to let me be taken for another.

ACT III

Scene 1

Don John in a Campaign Dress, Sganarelle dress'd like a Physician

SGANARELLE: Come, Sir, confess that I was in the right, and that we're both disguised to a Miracle. Your first Design was not at all proper; this conceals us much better than what you would ha' done.

DON JOHN: 'Tis true you're very well disguised; but I can't imagine where you discover'd that ridiculous Equipage.

SGANARELLE: 'Tis the Dress of an old Physician, which was left in Pawn in the Place where I had it; and it cost me Mony to get it. But do you know, Sir, that this Garment makes me a considerable Man? That I am saluted by those I meet with, and that I am consulted as if I were a skilful Man?

DON JOHN: How so?

SGANARELLE: Five or six Country People, seeing me go by, came to ask my Advice upon several Diseases.

DON JOHN: You answer'd 'em that you knew nothing of the Matter, ha?

SGANARELLE: No, not at all. I had a Mind to maintain the Honour of my Habit. I argued upon the Illness, and gave 'em a Prescription.

DON JOHN: And what Remedies did you prescribe?

SGANARELLE: Faith, Sir, I order'd 'em hap nap at a Venture, and 'twould be a comical Thing if the Patients should recover and come to thank me for't.

DON JOHN: And why not? Why should not you have the same Privilege as all other Physicians? They have no greater Share than you in the Cures of our Diseases, and all their Art is pure Grimace. They do nothing but receive the Glory of accidental Success, and you, like them, may make profit of the Fortune of the Patient, and see all that may proceed from the Favours of Chance or the Force of Nature attributed to your Remedies.

SGANARELLE: What, Sir, are you impious in Physick too?

DON JOHN: 'Tis one of greatest Errors that are amongst Men.

SGANARELLE: What! Have you no belief in Sena, Cassia, nor Emetic Wine?

DON JOHN: And why would you have me believe in 'em?

SGANARELLE: You have a heretick Soul. Yet you see what a Noise Emetic Wine has lately made in the World. Its Miracles have converted the most Incredulous, and 'tis not three Weeks ago since I, I that speak to you, beheld a wonderful Effect of it.

DON JOHN: And what was it?

SGANARELLE: There was a Man who for six Days lay a-dying. They could not tell what to give him, and all the Remedies did no good 'till at length they gave him Emetic.

DON JOHN: So he recover'd, ha?

SGANARELLE: No, he dy'd.

DON JOHN: Admirable Effect!

SGANARELLE: Why he could not die for six Days together, and that made him die 'pon the Spot. Would you have anything more effectual?

DON JOHN: You're in the Right.

SGANARELLE: But enough of Physick, which you ha' no belief in. Let's speak of other things, for this Habit inspires me with Wit, and I find myself in a Humour to dispute with you. You know you allow me to dispute, and forbid me nothing but Remonstrances!

DON JOHN: Well?

SGANARELLE: I'd fain know the bottom of your Thoughts, and be better acquainted with you than I am. Is't possible you have no Belief in Heaven at all?

DON JOHN: Leave this Matter.

SGANARELLE: You don't, in short. And in Hell?

DON JOHN: Eh!

SGANARELLE: The same. And in the Devil, if you please?

DON JOHN: Yes, yes.

SGANARELLE: As little. Have you no Belief in the Life hereafter?

DON JOHN: Ha! ha! ha!

SGANARELLE: Here's a man I will not easily convert. And tell me, what of the Bogy Man? Have you faith in him? Eh?

DON JOHN: A Plague on the Fool!

SGANARELLE: This is more than I can endure; for nothing is surer than the Bogy Man, and I wou'd go to the Stake for him. But a Man must have a Belief in this World. What is yours?

DON JOHN: What I believe?

SGANARELLE: Yes.

DON JOHN: I believe that two and two make four, Sganarelle, and four and four make eight.

SGANARELLE: A fine Creed! Handsome Articles of Faith! Your Religion, I see, is Arithmetik. It must be confess'd strange Follies enter the Heads of Men, and for all their Study they are often less wise than before. For my part, Sir, I have not study'd like you, thank

God, and no Man can boast he taught me anything; yet with my little Sense, my small Judgment, I see things better than all the Books, and I understand very well that the World which we see is not a Toadstool that came of itself one Night. Let me ask you who made those Trees, those Rocks, this Earth, and the Sky above you? Did it all come built of itself? Here, for example, you are yourself: did you make yourself alone? Was not your Father needed to beget you upon your Mother? Can you behold all the Inventions of which the human Machine consists without admiring how they conform together? These Nerves, these Bones, these Veins, these Arteries, this Heart, this Liver, this—these Lungs, and all the other Ingredients which—zounds, will you not interrupt me? I cannot dispute if I a'nt interrupted. You say nothing on Purpose, and allow me to speak from very Malice.

DON JOHN: I am waiting for the End of your Argument.

SGANARELLE: My Argument is that Man has something admirable, whate'er you may say, which all the learned Heads cannot explain. Is't not a Prodigy I shou'd be here, and have that in my Head which thinks a thousand different things in a Moment, and does with my Body all that it will? I want to clap my Hands, lift my Arm, raise my Eyes to the Sky, encline my Head, move my Feet, go to the right, to the left, forward, backward, turn—

[*He turns and falls.*]

DON JOHN: Good! There's your Argument with a broken Nose.

SGANARELLE: 'Sblood! I'm a Fool to reason with you. Believe what you will; 'tis nothing to me whether you be damn'd or no.

DON JOHN: While you reason'd, we lost our Way. Call that Man yonder and ask the Way of him.

Scene 2

Don John, Sganarelle, a Pauper

SGANARELLE: Ho there! Fellow! Ho! Mate! Ho! Friend! A little Word with you, if you please. Where lies our Way to the City?

PAUPER: Follow this Path, Gentlemen, and turn on your right Hand when you come to the Forest's end. But I warn you to be upon your Guard, for Robbers have been lurking of late in these Parts.

DON JOHN: I'm obliged to you, Friend, and thank you with all my Heart.

PAUPER: Will you help me, Sir, with a small Charity?

Don John: So! I see your Advice is selfish.

Pauper: Sir, I am a poor Man, retired for ten Years in the Solitude of this Forest, and I will not fail to pray that Heaven bestow upon you all Manner of Goods.

Don John: Eh! Ask Heaven for a Coat, without troubling yourself about other Men's Affairs.

Sganarelle: You don't know this Gentleman, my good Man; he believes only that two and two make four, and four and four make eight.

Don John: What is your Occupation amidst these Trees?

Pauper: To pray Heaven all Day that the kind Persons who succour me may thrive.

Don John: It cannot be, then, but you live comfortably here.

Pauper: Alas, Sir, I am as poor as can be.

Don John: Surely you jest. A Man who prays to Heaven all Day must be well furnish'd.

Pauper: I assure you, Sir, that I have often not a Crust to put into my Mouth.

Don John: Here is a strange thing, and your Efforts are but ill rewarded. Go to, I'll give you a Piece of Gold forthwith if you curse.

Pauper: Oh, Sir, wou'd you have me commit such a Sin?

Don John: Think only whether you wou'd earn a Piece of Gold or no. Here is one I'll give you if you curse. Here—but you must curse.

Pauper: Sir—

Don John: You shall not have it otherwise.

Sganarelle: Marry, swear a little; there's no Harm in't.

Don John: Take it, here, take it, I say; but curse away.

Pauper: No, Sir, I had rather starve.

Don John: Begone, I'll give it you for the love of Mankind. But what do I see? One Man set upon by three; the Match is too unequal, and I must not suffer so base a thing.

[*Runs to the place of Battle.*]

Scene 3

Don John, Don Carlos, Sganarelle

Sganarelle: Sure my Master is mad to run into a Danger he might have kept out of; but Faith, his help has done't, and the two have driven away the three.

Don Carlos [*with his Sword in his Hand*]: The flight of these Thieves

shews of what Consequence the help of your Arm is; let me return
you Thanks for so generous an Action, Sir, and—

DON JOHN: I have done nothing, Sir, but what you'd ha' done in my
Place. Our own Honour is concern'd in such Adventures, and the
Action of those Rogues was so base that not to have opposed 'em
would ha' been siding with 'em. But how came you to fall into their
Hands.

DON CARLOS: I lost my Brother and all our Followers by chance, and
as I was trying to get 'em again, I met with these Robbers, who
presently kill'd my Horse, and were it not for your Valour would
have done the same by me.

DON JOHN: Do you design to go towards the City?

DON CARLOS: Yes, but without going into it. My Brother and I are
obliged to travel for one of those troublesome Affairs which reduce
Gentlemen to sacrifice themselves and their Families to the Severity
of their Honour, since the best Success is always fatal, and since, if
they don't leave this Life, they're obliged to leave the Kingdom; and
in this I think the Condition of a Gentleman unfortunate, not to
be secure in the Prudence and Honesty of his own Conduct, but to
be subjected by the Laws of Honour to the Irregularity of another's,
and to see his Life, Repose and Estate depend upon the Whim of
the first rash Fellow that takes it in his Head to do him one of those
Injuries which an honest Man must perish for.

DON JOHN: We have the Advantage of making others run the same
Risk, and to give those who take a Fancy to offend us as much
Uneasiness. But would it not be an Indiscretion to ask what your
Affair may be?

DON CARLOS: The thing is to be made a Secret no longer, and when an
Injury is once publish'd, our Honour does not oblige us to conceal
our Shame, but rather to make our Revenge known and disclose our
Design of taking it. Therefore, Sir, I shall not scruple to tell you that
the Offence we seek Revenge for is a Sister's being seduced and
stol'n from a Nunnery, and that the Author of this Offence is one
Don John Tenorio, Son to Don Louis Tenorio. We have search'd
him for some Days, and we follow'd him this Morning upon the
Report of a Servant, who told us that he set out on Horseback accompany'd by four or five, and that he went by this Coast; but all
our Diligence was in vain, and we could not discover what's become
of him.

DON JOHN: Do you know this Don John whom you speak of, Sir?

DON CARLOS: I myself don't. I never saw him, and only heard him described by my Brother; but Report don't give him any of the best Characters, and 'tis a Man whose Life—

DON JOHN: Hold, Sir; he's one of my Friends, and 'twould be a kind of Baseness in me to hear any ill said of him.

DON CARLOS: For your sake, Sir, I'll say nothing of him; and the least thing I owe you, after you have saved my Life, is to say nothing in your Presence of one you are acquainted with when I can't speak well of him. But as much his Friend as you are, I hope you won't approve of his Action, nor think it strange that we seek Revenge for't.

DON JOHN: On the contrary, I'll serve you in it, and save your Labour; I am Don John's Friend, I can't help being so, but it is not reasonable that he should offend Gentlemen with Impunity; I'll engage myself to make him give you Satisfaction.

DON CARLOS: What Satisfaction can be done for such Injuries?

DON JOHN: All that your Honour can desire, and without giving you the Trouble to make any further search for Don John, I'll promise to bring him where and when you please.

DON CARLOS: This is very pleasant News, Sir, to offended Hearts; but after what I owe you, I should be uncommonly sorry if you were to be of the Party.

DON JOHN: There is that Intimacy between Don John and me that he can't fight but what I must fight too; but I answer for him as for myself, and you have no more to do than to tell me when you'd have him meet you and give you Satisfaction.

DON CARLOS: How cruel is my Destiny! Must I owe my Life to you, and Don John be one of your Friends?

Scene 4

Don Alonso and three Servants, Don Carlos, Don John, Sganarelle

DON ALONSO: Water my Horses, and bring 'em after us. I'll walk a little. O Heav'ns! What do I see! What! Brother, are you talking with our mortal Enemy?

DON CARLOS: Our mortal Enemy!

DON JOHN [*retiring back fiercely, laying his Hand upon his Sword*]: Yes, I myself am Don John, and the Advantage of Number shall not oblige me to conceal my Name.

DON ALONSO: Ah, Traitor, you must perish, and—

DON CARLOS: Hold, Brother, I owe my Life to him; without the Help of his Arm I should have been kill'd by some Thieves I met with.

DON ALONSO: Would you have that Consideration put a stop to our Revenge? The Services of an Enemy do not engage our Soul, and if you measure the Obligation against the Injury, your Gratitude is here ridiculous; and as Honour is infinitely more precious than Life, 'tis properly no Obligation to be obliged for Life to one that deprives us of our Honour.

DON CARLOS: I know the Difference, Brother, which a Gentleman ought always to make between one and t'other, and the Acknowledgement of the Obligation does not blot out my Resentment of the Injury. But let me now repay him what he has lent me. Let me acquit myself upon the Spot for the Life I owe him by delaying our Revenge, and give him the Liberty of enjoying for a few Days the Fruit of his Kindness.

DON ALONSO: No, 'tis hazarding our Revenge to defer it, and the Opportunity of taking him may not come again; Heaven now offers it, and we ought to improve the Occasion. When Honour is mortally wounded, one ought to keep no Measure, and if you are not willing to lend your Arm to the Action, you may begone, and leave to my Hand the Glory of such a sacrifice.

DON CARLOS: Pray, Brother—

DON ALONSO: All you can say's superfluous; he must die.

DON CARLOS: Hold, I say, Brother. I won't see his Life attack'd and I swear I'll defend him against anyone, be it who it will, and will guard him with the same Life he has saved. To address your Blows, you must kill me first.

DON ALONSO: What! Do you side with our Enemy against me, and instead of being seized at his Aspect with the same Transports that I am, do you shew Sentiments full of Mercy for him?

DON CARLOS: Brother, let's be moderate, and not Revenge our Honour with so much Rage. Let's have an Heart that we can master, a Valour without Savageness, and which does things by a pure Deliberation of our Reason, and not by the Instigation of a blind Passion. I won't remain obliged to my Enemy; I must acquit myself of my Obligation to him before I do anything else. Though our Revenge be defer'd, it will be ne'er the less exemplary; on the contrary 'twill be the greater, and this Opportunity, not taken, will make it appear the juster in the Eyes of the whole World.

DON ALONSO: O strange Weakness! Thus to hazard the Interests of your Honour for the ridiculous Thought of a chimerical Obligation!

DON CARLOS: No, Brother, don't disturb yourself. If I commit a Fault I am able to repair it, and I take upon me the whole Care of our Honour; I know what that obliges us to do, and the Delay of a Day, which my Gratitude imposes, will but augment my Impatience to satisfy it. Don John, you see how careful I am to restore you the Good I have received from you, and by that you may imagine that I shall acquit myself of my Duty with the same Warmth, and that I shall be no less exact to repay you the Injury than the Kindness. I won't oblige you now to express your Sentiments, and I give you the Liberty to think at your leisure of the Resolutions you are to take. You are sufficiently acquainted with the greatness of the Offence you have committed, and I make you yourself Judge of the Reparations it requires. There are peaceful Means to satisfy us; there are likewise violent and bloody ones. But make what Choice you will, you have given me your Word to make Don John satisfie me; pray take care to do it, and remember that, away from this Place, I owe no Obligation except to my Honour.

DON JOHN: I required nothing of you, and shall keep my Promise.

DON CARLOS: Come, Brother, a Moment's Forbearance does not injure the Severity of our Duty.

Scene 5

Don John, Sganarelle

DON JOHN: So ho, Sganarelle.

SGANARELLE: Anon!

DON JOHN: What, Knave, do you run away when I'm attack'd?

SGANARELLE: I beg your Pardon, Sir, I was hard by; I believe this Dress is Purgative, and that to wear it is as good as a Potion.

DON JOHN: Plague take your Insolence! Cover your Cowardice with a more honourable Veil at least. Do you know who he is whose Life I saved?

SGANARELLE: No, not I.

DON JOHN: 'Tis a Brother of Elvira's.

SGANARELLE: A—

DON JOHN: He is a good honest Man; he was not ungrateful, and I'm sorry I have a Quarrel with him.

SGANARELLE: 'Twou'd be easy for you to pacifie things.

DON JOHN: Yes, but my Passion for Donna Elvira is worn out, and the

Engagement does not at all agree with my Humour. I am for Liberty in Love, you know it, and cannot bear to confine my Heart within four Walls. I have told you twenty times that I have a natural Inclination to give way to whatever attracts me. My Heart belongs to all the Fair Sex, and they're to take it by turns, and keep it as long as they can. But what lofty Edifice do I see amongst those Trees?

SGANARELLE: Don't you know?

DON JOHN: No, truly.

SGANARELLE: Why 'tis the Tomb the Governor was making when you kill'd him.

DON JOHN: You're in the right. I did not know that 'twas hereabouts. Everybody speaks Wonders of this Work, as well as of the Governor's Statue; I have a mind to go see it.

SGANARELLE: Sir, don't go.

DON JOHN: Why not?

SGANARELLE: 'Tis not civil to go see a Man that you kill'd.

DON JOHN: On the contrary, 'tis a Visit I'll make him out of Civility, and which he ought to receive graciously if he's a Gallant Man. Come, let's go in.

[*The Tomb opens, and on the inside is a stately Mausoleum and the* STATUE OF THE GOVERNOR.]

SGANARELLE: O how fine this is! Fine Statues! Fine Marble! Fine Pillars! How fine this is! What do you think on't, Sir?

DON JOHN: That the Ambition of a dead Man cou'd not reach further; and what I think most wonderful is that a Man who in his Lifetime took up with a simple Habitation shou'd desire so magnificent a house when he can no longer enjoy it.

SGANARELLE: Here's the Governor's Statue.

DON JOHN: Zoons, there he is with the Habit of a Roman Emperor.

SGANARELLE: Faith, Sir, 'tis finely made. It looks as if it were alive and were going to speak. He gives us such Looks as wou'd frighten me if I were alone; I think he e'nt pleas'd to see us.

DON JOHN: He's in the wrong then, and 'twou'd be an ill Reception of the Honour that I bestow upon him. Ask him if he'll come and Sup with me.

SGANARELLE: 'Tis a thing he has no need of, I think.

DON JOHN: Ask him, I tell you.

SGANARELLE: Do you Jest? 'Twou'd be a piece of Folly to speak to a Statue.

DON JOHN: Do as I bid you.

SGANARELLE: What Extravagance this is! Sir Governor—I can't help laughing at my Folly, but my Master makes me do it—Sir Governor, my Master Don John desires to know if you'll do him the Honour to come and Sup with him. [*The* STATUE *nods.*] Ha!

DON JOHN: What's the matter? What ails you? Speak.

SGANARELLE [*makes the same Sign the Statue had made to him, and nods*]: The Statue—

DON JOHN: What do you mean, Villain?

SGANARELLE: I tell you the Statue—

DON JOHN: What of the Statue? I'll break your Bones unless you speak.

SGANARELLE: The Statue nodded to me.

DON JOHN: Plague take the Knave!

SGANARELLE: He nodded to me, I tell you; nothing's more certain. Go speak to him yourself, and see—

DON JOHN: Come, Rogue, come, I'll shew you your Cowardice. Watch me. Will the Lord Governor come and Sup with me?

[STATUE *nods again.*]

SGANARELLE: I'd give ten Pounds for this. Well, Sir?

DON JOHN: Come, let's be gone.

SGANARELLE: These are your Free-thinkers that will believe nothing.

ACT IV

Scene 1

Don John, Sganarelle, Ragotin

DON JOHN: Be it as it will, no more of that. 'Tis a Trifle, and we might have been deceived by a false Light, or surprized by some Vapour which disturb'd our Eyes.

SGANARELLE: O, Sir, don't try to contradict that which we have seen with these very Eyes. Nothing can be more certain than the Nod of the Head, and I don't doubt but Heaven, offended with your Life, produced this Miracle to convince you, and to reclaim you from—

DON JOHN: Do you hear? If you trouble me any more with your foolish Morality, if you say the least Word to me about it, I'll call somebody, get a Bull's Pizzle, have you held by three or four, and break your Bones. Do you hear me?

SGANARELLE: Very well, Sir, mighty well, you express yourself plain enough; that's one good thing in you, you never seek for Shifts, you say things with an admirable Clearness.

DON JOHN: Come, let me have my Supper as soon as possible. A Chair, Boy.

Scene 2

Don John, Violette, Sganarelle, Ragotin

VIOLETTE: Sir, here's your Tradesman, Mr. Sunday, wants to speak with you.

SGANARELLE: Ay, we wanted a Creditor's Compliment. What cou'd put it in his head to come to ask us for Mony; and why did not you tell him that my Master was not at home?

VIOLETTE: I have told him so for these three Quarters of an Hour; but he wou'd not believe it and sat down without to wait.

SGANARELLE: Let him wait as long as he will.

DON JOHN: No, on the contrary, bid him come in; 'tis very ill Politicks to conceal oneself from Creditors. 'Tis good to pay 'em with something, and I have the Art of sending 'em away satisfy'd without giving 'em a Farthing.

Scene 3

Don John, Mr. Sunday, Sganarelle, Servants

DON JOHN [*with a great deal of Civility*]: O Mr. Sunday, come hither. How glad am I to see you, and how angry I am with my People for not letting you come in before! I order'd 'em, indeed, to deny me to everybody, but that Order did not extend to you; you have a right always to find my Door open.

MR. SUNDAY: Sir, I'm very much obliged to you.

DON JOHN [*to his Lacquies*]: Rascals, I'll teach you to leave Mr. Sunday in an Antichamber; I'll make you know People.

MR. SUNDAY: Sir, 'tis nothing.

DON JOHN: What, to deny me to Mr. Sunday, the best of my Friends?

MR. SUNDAY: Sir, I'm your Servant. I came to—

DON JOHN: Come, a Chair for Mr. Sunday, quickly.

MR. SUNDAY: Sir, I'm very well as I am.

DON JOHN: No, no, I'll have you sit down by me.

MR. SUNDAY: There's no need on't.

DON JOHN: Take away that Stool, and bring an Armchair.

MR. SUNDAY: Sir, you jest, and—

DON JOHN: No, no, I know what I owe you, and will make no Difference between us two.

MR. SUNDAY: Sir—

DON JOHN: Come, sit down.

MR. SUNDAY: There's no need on't, Sir: I have but one word to say to you. I was—

DON JOHN: Sit down, I say.

MR. SUNDAY: No, Sir, I am very well; I came to—

DON JOHN: No, I won't hear you unless you sit down.

MR. SUNDAY: Sir, I do as you'll have me. I—

DON JOHN: Faith, Mr. Sunday, you look very hearty and jolly.

MR. SUNDAY: Yes, Sir, at your Service. I come—

DON JOHN: You have an admirable Constitution, fresh Lips, a cherry Colour, and brisk Eyes.

MR. SUNDAY: I wou'd fain—

DON JOHN: How does Madam Sunday your Wife do?

MR. SUNDAY: Very well, Sir, thank God.

DON JOHN: She's a fine Woman.

MR. SUNDAY: She's your Servant, Sir. I came to—

DON JOHN: And how does your little Daughter Claudine?

MR. SUNDAY: Mighty well.

DON JOHN: What a pretty little Girl 'tis! I love her with all my Heart.

MR. SUNDAY: You do her too much Honour, Sir. I—

DON JOHN: And does little Colin make a Noise with his Drum still?

MR. SUNDAY: Yes, Sir. I—

DON JOHN: And your little Dog, Basquet? Does he bark as he us'd to do, and bite People's Legs?

MR. SUNDAY: More than ever, Sir, and we can't break him of it.

DON JOHN: Don't wonder if I inquire so much about your Family, for I concern myself mightily in it.

MR. SUNDAY: We're infinitely obliged to you, Sir. I—

DON JOHN [*holding his Hand to him*]: Give me your Hand, Mr. Sunday. Are you my Friend?

MR. SUNDAY: Sir, I'm your Servant.

DON JOHN: Faith, I'm yours with all my Heart.

MR. SUNDAY: You Honour me too much. I—

DON JOHN: There's nothing that I wou'd not do for you.

MR. SUNDAY: Sir, you have too much Goodness for me.

DON JOHN: I hope you'll believe it's without Selfishness too.

MR. SUNDAY: I have not deserved this Favour; but, Sir—

DON JOHN: Hark, Mr. Sunday, will you sup with me? Come, no Compliments.

MR. SUNDAY: No, Sir, I must be gone presently. I—

DON JOHN [*rising*]: Come, a Torch, quickly, to light Mr. Sunday, and let four or five of my People take Musketoons to guard him.

MR. SUNDAY [*rising too*]: Sir, there's no need on't; I can go very well alone. But—

[SGANARELLE *takes away the Chairs hastily.*]

DON JOHN: What? You shall be guarded; I interest myself in your Person, and am both your Servant and Debtor.

MR. SUNDAY: O Sir—

DON JOHN: 'Tis a thing I won't conceal, and I tell it the whole World.

MR. SUNDAY: If—

DON JOHN: Give me leave to wait upon you to the Door.

MR. SUNDAY: O Sir, you're pleas'd to be merry. Sir—

DON JOHN: Embrace me then; I beg you once more to be persuaded that I am entirely yours, and that there's nothing that I wou'd not do to serve you.

[*Exit.*]

SGANARELLE: I must own you have in my Master a Man that has a great Kindness for you.

MR. SUNDAY: 'Tis true he uses so much Civility and Ceremony that I can never ask him for my Money.

SGANARELLE: I assure you he'd destroy his whole Family for you, and I wish something wou'd but happen to you, that somebody wou'd cudgel you, you shou'd see how—

MR. SUNDAY: I believe it; but Sganarelle, pray put him in mind of my Money.

SGANARELLE: O don't be disturb'd about it. He'll pay extreamely well.

MR. SUNDAY: But you, Sganarelle, owe me something yourself.

SGANARELLE: Fie, don't speak of it.

MR. SUNDAY: Why, I—

SGANARELLE: Don't I know what I owe you?

MR. SUNDAY: Yes, but—

SGANARELLE: Come, Mr. Sunday, I'll light you.

MR. SUNDAY: But my Money—

SGANARELLE [*taking Mr. Sunday by the Arm*]: You jest.

MR. SUNDAY: I will—

SGANARELLE [*pulling him*]: Eh!

MR. SUNDAY: I mean—

SGANARELLE [*pushing him*]: Trifles!

MR. SUNDAY: But—

SGANARELLE [*pushing him*]: Fie.

MR. SUNDAY: I—

SGANARELLE [*pushing him quite off the Stage*]: Fie, I say.

Scene 4

Don Louis, Don John, Violette, Sganarelle

VIOLETTE: Sir, here's your Father.

DON JOHN: This Visit is all that was wanting to make me mad.

DON LOUIS: I see I disturb you, and that you cou'd very gladly have dispensed with this Visit. 'Tis true we're strangely troublesome to each other, and if you are uneasie at my Sight, I am very uneasie at your Conduct. Alas, how little do we know what we do when we do not leave to Heaven the Care of what is necessary for us, when we would be wiser than it, and importune it by our blind Wishes and inconsiderate Requests! I wish'd for a Son with unparallel'd Ardour; I incessantly pray'd for one with incredible Transports; and the Son which Heaven has granted me is the Grief and Punishment of this same Life which I thought he must comfort and rejoice. With what Eye do you think I can behold that Series of unworthy Actions which we have much ado to show the World with a fair Countenance; that continual Train of wicked Affairs which daily reduces us to tire the Goodness of our Sovereign, and which has exhausted the Merit of my Services and the Credit of my Friends? O what Baseness is this! Do you not blush to be so little deserving of your Birth? Do you think you have any right now to boast of it? What have you done in the World to be call'd a Gentleman? Do you believe 'tis enough to bear the Name and Arms of one, and that 'tis a Glory to be sprung of noble Blood when a Man lives like an infamous Wretch? No, no, Birth is nothing where Virtue is wanting. We have no further share in the Glory of our Ancestors than as we endeavour to resemble them, and the Lustre of their Actions, which they spread over us, impose on us a Duty to do them the same Honour, to follow the Examples they give us, and not to degenerate from their Virtues if we would be esteem'd their true Descendants. Thus in vain you descend from the Ancestors you spring from; they disown you for their Blood, and all their illustrious Actions give you no Advantage. On the contrary, their Fame is your Dishonour, and their Glory lights to everyone's Eyes the Shame of your Actions. In short, know that a Gentleman that lives ill is a Monster in Nature; that Virtue is the first Degree of Nobility; that I esteem a Name much less than Actions, and that I should have more regard for the Son of a Porter that was an honest Man than the Son of a Monarch that should live like you.

DON JOHN: Sir, if you'd sit down you might talk with greater ease.

DON LOUIS: No, Insolence, I won't sit down, nor speak any more; I see that all my Words have no effect upon you. But know, unworthy Son, that a Father's tenderness is spent by your Actions, that, sooner than you imagine, I shall put a stop to your Irregularities, prevent the Wrath of Heaven upon you, and by your Punishment wash away the Shame of having begotten you.

[*Exit.*]

Scene 5

Don John, Sganarelle

DON JOHN: Die as soon as you can; that's the best thing you can do. Every Dog must have his Day, and it makes me mad to see Fathers live as long as their Sons.

[*Sits down in his Chair.*]

SGANARELLE: O Sir, you're in the wrong.

DON JOHN: In the wrong?

SGANARELLE: Sir—

DON JOHN [*Rising*]: In the wrong?

SGANARELLE: Yes, Sir, you were in the wrong to hear him; you ought to have turn'd him out by Neck and Shoulders. Was ever anything more Impertinent? A Father to make Remonstrances to his Son, and to bid him correct his Actions, remember his Birth, lead the Life of a Man of Honour, and an hundred other Follies of the like Nature? Is that to be borne by such a Man as you, who knows how to live? I admire your Patience, and had I been in your Place, I should ha' sent him packing. [*Aside.*] O damn'd Compliance, to what dost thou reduce me!

DON JOHN: Is Supper ready?

Scene 6

Don John, Donna Elvira, Ragotin, Sganarelle

RAGOTIN: Sir, here's a Lady in a Veil that comes to speak with you.

DON JOHN: Who can it be?

SGANARELLE: We must see.

DONNA ELVIRA: Don't be surpris'd, Don John, to see me at this Hour, and in this Equipage. A pressing Motive obliges me to make this Visit, and what I have to say to you will admit of no delay. I don't now come in the Anger that I shew'd before; I am changed from what I was this Morning. 'Tis no more that Donna Elvira who pray'd against you, and whose irritated Soul utter'd nothing but Threats and breathed Revenge only. Heaven has banish'd from my soul all the unworthy Ardour I had for you, all the tumultuous Transports of a criminal Affection, all the shameful Passions of a gross and earthly Love, and it has left in my Heart a Flame refined from all commerce of the Senses, a Tenderness entirely holy, a Love abstracted from everything, and acting not for itself but for your Interest only.

DON JOHN [to Sganarelle]: You weep, I think?

SGANARELLE: Excuse me.

DONNA ELVIRA: 'Tis that perfect and pure Love which brings me hither for your Good, to impart to you an Advice from Heaven, and try to preserve you from the Precipice you are running into. Yes, Don John, I am acquainted with all the Irregularities of your Life, and that same Heav'n which has touch'd my Heart and made me consider the Errors of my Conduct, inspired me to come to you and to tell you on its behalf that your Offences have exhausted its Mercy; that its terrible Indignation is ready to fall upon you; that it lies in your Power to prevent it by a speedy Repentance, and that perhaps you have not a Day longer to save yourself from the greatest of Misfortunes. For my part, I am not ty'd to you any longer by any worldly Affection. Thank Heav'n, I am recover'd from foolish Thoughts; my Retreat is resolv'd upon, and I only desire Life enough to expiate the Fault I have committed, and merit by an austere Penance a Pardon for the Blindness into which the Transports of a blameable Passion plunged me. But in this Retreat I should be extremely sorry that a Person whom I had cherished so tenderly should become a fatal Example of Heaven's Justice, and 'twould be an incredible Joy to me if I could prevail upon you to ward off the terrible Blow that threatens you. Pray, Don John, grant me as the last Favour this sweet Comfort; don't refuse me your Salvation which I request with Tears, and if you yourself are not concern'd for your own Interest, yet be so for my Desires at least. Don't let me have the cruel Mortification of seeing you condemn'd to eternal Punishments.

SGANARELLE: Poor Woman!

DONNA ELVIRA: I have loved you with an extream Tenderness; nothing in the World was so dear to me as you have been. I forgot my Duty for you, I have done everything for you, and all the Recompence I desire is that you'd correct your Life and prevent your Destruction. I beg you to save yourself, either for your own sake or mine. Once more, Don John, I desire it with Tears, and if the Tears of a Person you have loved be not sufficient, I conjure you to do it by all that is most capable of touching you.

SGANARELLE [*Aside*.]: Tyger!

DONNA ELVIRA: Now I am gone; this is all I had to say to you.

DON JOHN: Madam, 'tis late, stay here; we'll get as good a Lodging for you as we can.

DONNA ELVIRA: No, Don John, don't keep me any longer.

DON JOHN: Madam, I assure you you'd oblige me if you'd stay.

DONNA ELVIRA: No, I tell you, don't let us lose time in superfluous Discourse; let me go quickly, don't wait upon me, and think of nothing but profiting by my Advice.

Scene 7

Don John, Sganarelle; Don John's Servants

DON JOHN: Do you know that I still felt a little Emotion for her; that I found this whimsical Novelty agreeable, and that her negligent Habit, her languishing Air, and her Tears awaken'd in me some few Remains of an extinguish'd Flame?

SGANARELLE: That's as much as to say her Words had no effect upon you?

DON JOHN: Come; Supper, quickly.

SGANARELLE: Very well.

DON JOHN [*sitting down to Table*]: Still, Sganarelle, we must think of reforming.

SGANARELLE: Ay, marry, we must.

DON JOHN: Yes, Faith, we must reform; we'll live thus for twenty or thirty Years longer, and then we'll take care of ourselves.

SGANARELLE: Oh!

DON JOHN: What do you say to't?

SGANARELLE: Nothing; here comes Supper.

[*He takes a bit out of one of the Plates, before it comes to Table, and claps it in his Mouth.*]

DON JOHN: Your Cheek seems to be swell'd. What is't? Speak, what's i' your Mouth?

SGANARELLE: Nothing.

DON JOHN: Let's see; Zoons, 'tis a Fluxion that's fallen into his Cheek; quick, a Lancet to cut it. The poor Fellow can't live long, and this Impostume may choak him; stay, let's see whether 'tis ripe. Ah Sirrah!

SGANARELLE: Faith, Sir, I had a mind to taste if your Cook had not overseason'd it.

DON JOHN: Come, sit down and eat. I have something for you to do after Supper. I see you are hungry.

SGANARELLE [*Sits down.*]: 'Tis true, Sir; I han't eat since Morning. Taste this; it's mighty good. [*A Lacquey takes away Sganarelle's Plate so soon as ever he has put anything upon it.*] My Plate, my Plate. Soft and fair, if you please. Faith, Brother, how skilful you are in giving me empty Plates; and you, little Violette, how well you know when to give Drink. [*Whilst one Lacquey gives Sganarelle Drink, t'other takes away his Plate again.*]

DON JOHN: Who knocks so hard?

SGANARELLE: Who the Devil comes to trouble us at our Meals?

DON JOHN: I'll sup in quiet; let nobody come in.

SGANARELLE: Let me see to it. I'll go to the Door myself.

DON JOHN: What's the Matter? Who's there?

SGANARELLE: The—[*He nods as the Statue did.*]—is there.

DON JOHN: I'll see him, and shew that nothing can shake me.

SGANARELLE: O poor Sganarelle, where wilt thou hide thyself!

Scene 8

Don John, the GOVERNOR'S STATUE *which goes and sits down to Table; Sganarelle, and Servants.*

DON JOHN: A Chair and a Plate, quickly. [*To Sganarelle.*] Come, sit down.

SGANARELLE: Sir, I e'nt a hungry now.

DON JOHN: Sit you down, I say. Drink here. Here's the Governor's Health, Sganarelle. Give him some Wine.

SGANARELLE: Sir, I'm not thirsty.

DON JOHN: Drink, and sing your Song to make the Governor merry.

SGANARELLE: I have a Cold, Sir.

DON JOHN: 'Tis no matter, come. Do you there come and join his Voice.

STATUE: Don John, 'tis enough. I invite you to come and sup with me tomorrow. Shall you be bold enough?

DON JOHN: Yes, I'll come accompany'd by none but Sganarelle.

SGANARELLE: I thank you, but I fast tomorrow.

DON JOHN [*to Sganarelle*]: Here, take this Torch.

STATUE: Those that are conducted by Heav'n have no need of Light.

ACT V

Scene 1

Don Louis, Don John, Sganarelle

DON LOUIS: What, Son, is it possible that Heav'n's Goodness has heard my Prayers? Is what you tell me true? Don't you abuse me with a false Hope, and may I believe the surprizing Novelty of such a Conversion?

DON JOHN [*playing the Hypocrite*]: Yes, I am return'd from all my Errors. I am not the same as I was Yesterday Evening, and Heav'n has all of a sudden work'd a Change in me which will surprize everybody. It has touch'd my Heart and open'd my Eyes, and with Horror I look back upon the long Blindness I have been in and the disorderly Life I have led. I consider all the Abominations of it, and am amaz'd how Heav'n cou'd so long endure 'em, and has not twenty times let fall upon my Head the Blows of its terrible Justice. I see the Favour its Goodness has done me in not punishing me for my Crimes, and I intend to profit as I ought; to shew the World a sudden Alteration of my Life, thereby to repair the Scandal of my past Actions, and to endeavour to obtain of Heav'n a full Forgiveness. This I'll go about, and I beg you, Sir, to contribute to the Design and to help me yourself to a Person that may be my Guide, and under whose Conduct I may walk securely into the Journey I am undertaking.

DON LOUIS: O Son, how easily is a Father's Tenderness recall'd, and how a Child's Offences are immediately wash'd away by the least mention of Repentance. I now forget all the Uneasiness you have given me, and all is effaced by the Words you have spoken. I confess I am not myself. I shed Tears for Joy, all my Desires are satisfy'd, and I have no more to ask of Heav'n. Embrace me, my Son, and

I conjure you, persist in this laudable Resolution. I'll immediately go tell this happy News to your Mother, share with her the sweet Transports of the Rapture I am in, and thank Heav'n for the holy Thoughts it has been pleased to inspire you with.

Scene 2

Don John, Sganarelle

SGANARELLE: O, Sir, how glad am I to see you converted! I have long expected this, and now, thank Heav'n, all my Wishes are accomplish'd.

DON JOHN: Plague take the Ass!

SGANARELLE: How! The Ass!

DON JOHN: What; do you take all I said for current Coyn, and do you think that my Mouth is in Concert with my Heart?

SGANARELLE: What, is not—don't you—your—O what a Man this is! What a Man this is!

DON JOHN: No, no, I'm not at all changed, and my Sentiments are still the same.

SGANARELLE: Don't you yield to the surprising Marvel of that Statue, both moving and speaking?

DON JOHN: There's something in that indeed which I don't comprehend; but be it as 'twill, that is not capable either to convince my Mind or shake my Soul; and if I said I would mend my Conduct and lead an exemplary Life, 'twas a Design I form'd out of pure Policy, a useful Stratagem, a necessary Grimace which I'll constrain myself to, to manage a Father whom I have need of, and to be secure from an hundred Accidents which may happen to me from Men. I entrust you with this Secret, Sganarelle, and I'm glad that I've a Witness of the real Motives which instigate me to do Things.

SGANARELLE: What! Still an Unbeliever, and yet pretend to Godliness?

DON JOHN: And why not? There are a great many besides me that practice that Trade, and who make use of the same Mask to abuse the World.

SGANARELLE: Oh! What a Man! What a Man!

DON JOHN: There's no shame in this now; Hypocrisie is a fashionable Vice, and all fashionable Vices pass for Virtues. The Part of an honest Man is the best a Man can play. The Profession of an Hypocrite has wonderful Advantages today. 'Tis an Art whose Imposture is always respected, and tho' 'tis discover'd, nobody dares speak against it. All Men's other Vices are exposed to Censure, and each has the Liberty of attacking them openly; but Hypocrisie is a privileged Vice which with its Hand stops everyone's Mouth and enjoys in quiet an absolute Impunity. One contracts, by means of this Grimace, a strict Friendship with all the Professors of it. He that offends one, pulls 'em all upon him; and those who act sincerely in it, and whom everyone knows to be really touch'd, those, I say, are generally the Dupes to the others; they are easily gull'd by the Grimacers, and blindly support the Apes of their Actions. How many are there who by this Stratagem have cunningly to my Knowledge made up for the Disorders of their Youth, who make a Shield of Religion's Coat, and under a respectful Outside have Liberty to be the wicked'st Fellows in the World? 'Tis no matter if their Intrigues be publish'd and they be known for what they are; they are ne'er the less in Credit, and a little hanging down of the Head, a mortify'd Groan, and two Turnings up of the Eyes set all to rights again. Under this favourable Covert I intend to secure my Affairs. I won't leave off my beloved Customs, but I'll take care to conceal myself and take Diversion privately. But if I come to be discover'd, my Part will be taken by all the League without my stirring in it, and I shall be defended by them against everybody. In short, this is the true way to do all I have a Mind to with Impunity. I'll set up for a Censor of the Actions of others, judge ill of all the World, and have a good Opinion of none but myself. If anyone offends me ever so little, I'll never forgive, but demurely preserve an irreconcileable Hatred. I'll be the Avenger of Heaven's Interests, and under that commodious Pretence I'll pursue my Enemies, accuse 'em of Impiety, and halloo at 'em the indiscreet Zealots, who without knowing the Reason will cry out against 'em, load 'em with Injuries, and by their own private Authority pronounce Damnation against 'em. Thus Men's Weakness must be profited by, and thus a wise Man will accommodate himself to the Vices of his Age.

SGANARELLE: O Heav'ns! What do I hear! Hypocrisie was all that was wanting to finish you quite, and this is the full Measure of Abominations. Sir, this last Stroke provokes me, and I can't help speaking. Do what you please to me, beat me, break my Bones, murther me if you will, I must disburthen my Heart, and like a faithful Servant tell you what I ought. Know, Sir, that a Pitcher never goes so often to the Well but it comes home broke at last, and as that Author, tho' I don't know who 'tis, very well says, Man in this World is like a Bird on a Bough; the Bough is fix'd to the Tree; he that is fix'd to the Tree follows good Precepts; good Precepts are better than fair Words; fair Words are found at Court; at Court are Courtiers; the Courtiers follow the Fashion; Fashion proceeds from the Fancy; the Fancy is a Faculty of the Soul; the Soul is what gives us Life; Life ends in Death; Death puts us in Mind of Heaven; Heaven is above the Earth; the Earth is not the Sea; the Sea is subject to Storms; Storms torment Vessels; Vessels need a good Pilot; a good Pilot is prudent; Prudence is not in the Young; the Young must obey the Old; the Old love Riches; Riches make rich Men; rich Men are not poor; the Poor are in Need; Need hath no Law; whoever has no Law lives as a brute Beast; and, in consequence, you shall be damn'd to all the Devils.

DON JOHN: A fine Argument, truly!

SGANARELLE: If this won't convince you, so much the worse for you.

Scene 3

Don Carlos, Don John, Sganarelle

DON CARLOS: Don John, I meet you very seasonably, and had rather speak to you here than at your Lodgings to ask you your Resolutions. You know that Care concerns me, and I in your Presence took this Affair upon me. For my Part, I don't conceal it, I should be glad if things could be adjusted peaceably, and there's nothing I wou'd not do to prevail with you to take that Course, and to see my Sister publickly confirm'd by you in the Title of your Wife.

DON JOHN [*in a canting Tone*]: Alas! I would with all my Heart give you the Satisfaction you desire, but Heaven directly opposes it; it has inspired my Soul with a Desire to change my Life, and I have now no other Thought than to quit entirely all worldly Things, to lay aside as soon as possible all manner of Vanity, and henceforth to correct, by an austere Conduct, all the criminal Irregularities which the Heat of blind Youth hurry'd me into.

DON CARLOS: This design, Don John, does not run counter with what I say, and the Company of a lawful Wife may be very agreeable to the laudable Thoughts Heav'n inspires you with.

DON JOHN: Alas! not at all; 'tis a Design your Sister too has form'd; she is resolved to retire, and we were both touch'd at the same time.

DON CARLOS: Her Retirement cannot satisfie us because it may be imputed to your Contempt of her and our Family, and our Honour requires that she should live with you.

DON JOHN: I assure you, it cannot be. I was very desirous of it, and this very Day consulted Heav'n about it; but when I consulted it, I heard a Voice which told me that I ought not to think of your Sister, and that I could never work out my Salvation in her Company.

DON CARLOS: Do you think these fair Excuses will blind us, Don John?

DON JOHN: I obey the Voice of Heav'n.

DON CARLOS: What! Would you have me be contented with such a Story?

DON JOHN: Heav'n will have it so.

DON CARLOS: Did you take my Sister out of a Nunnery to leave her at last?

DON JOHN: Heav'n ordains it so.

DON CARLOS: Shall we bear this Blot upon our Family?

DON JOHN: Blame Heaven for it.

DON CARLOS: What? Nothing but Heav'n?

DON JOHN: Heav'n will have it so.

DON CARLOS: 'Tis enough, Don John, I understand you; I won't take you here, the Place won't admit of it; but before long I shall meet with you.

DON JOHN: You may do as you please. You know I don't want a Heart, and that I can make use of my Sword when there's need for't; I'll go walk presently in that little bye Street which leads to the Convent; but for my Part, I declare that 'tis not I that wou'd fight; Heav'n forbids that I should have such a Thought, and if you attack me, we shall see what will be the Consequence.

DON CARLOS: 'Tis true, we shall see, we shall see.

Scene 4

Don John, Sganarelle

SGANARELLE: What a dev'lish Stile do you use, Sir! This is worse than all the rest, and I'd rather have you as you were before. I always had

Hopes of your Salvation, but now I despair of it, and I believe that Heav'n, which hitherto has endured you, cannot bear this last Abomination.

DON JOHN: Pish, Heav'n is not so strict as you imagine, and if as often as Men—

SGANARELLE [*Seeing the Ghost*]: Oh Sir, 'tis Heav'n that speaks to you; and 'tis a Warning it gives you.

DON JOHN: If Heav'n gives me Warning, it must speak plainer if 'twou'd have me understand it.

Scene 5

Don John, Sganarelle, a Ghost in the form of a Woman veil'd

GHOST: Don John has but a Moment's time to lay hold on the Mercy of Heav'n, and if he do not repent now, his Destruction is certain.

SGANARELLE: Do you hear, Sir?

DON JOHN: Who dares to say this? I think I know the Voice.

SGANARELLE: Oh, Sir, 'tis a Ghost, I know it by its walking.

DON JOHN: Ghost, Phantom, or Devil, I'll see what 'tis.

[*The* GHOST *changes its Figure, and represents Time with a Scythe in its Hand.*]

SGANARELLE: O Heav'ns! Do you see this Metamorphosis, Sir?

DON JOHN: No, no, nothing is capable of terrifying me, and with my Sword I'll try whether 'tis a Body or a Spirit.

[*The* SPIRIT *vanishes when Don John offers to strike it.*]

SGANARELLE: O Sir, yield to so many Proofs, and fall to Repentance quickly.

DON JOHN: No, no, come what will, it shall never be said that I was capable of Repentance. Follow me.

Scene 6

The Statue, Don John, Sganarelle

STATUE: Stay, Don John. Yesterday you gave me your Word to come and eat with me.

DON JOHN: I did; where must I go?

STATUE: Give me your Hand.

DON JOHN: There 'tis.

STATUE: Don John, Obstinacy in Wickedness brings on a fatal Death; and Heaven's Mercy rejected opens away for its Thunder.

DON JOHN: O Heav'ns, what do I feel! An invisible Flame consumes me; I can bear it no longer; all my Body is a burning Firebrand. Oh—

[*Thunder and Lightning, with a great noise, fall upon* DON JOHN, *the Earth opens and swallows him up, and Great Flames rise from the Place he sunk into.*]

SCANARELLE: Ha! My Wages! My Wages! Now is everybody satisfy'd by his Death. Offended Heav'n, violated Laws, seduced Daughters, dishonour'd Families, abused Parents, Wives reduced to Misery, Husbands to Desperation, ev'rybody is contented; I alone am miserable. My Wages, my Wages, my Wages!

LORENZO DA PONTE

The Punished Libertine

or

Don Giovanni

A Comic Drama in Two Acts

(1787)

Translated by Adrienne Schizzano Mandel
and Oscar Mandel

TRANSLATORS' NOTE

This translation attempts in principle to present Da Ponte's work not as the libretto of an opera, but as an actable play with or without incidental musical accompaniment. A few liberties have therefore been taken with the text as it appears in the operatic score. Arias which exist *only* for the sake of the music have been omitted or condensed. Repetitions, effective in music but clearly out of place in spoken drama, are eliminated unless they are dramatically useful. The texts of ensembles are either assigned to the single actors they suit best, or distributed to several. Minor modifications in dialogue and action are made in order to rationalize the work as, for example, in Act II, Scene 4, where Ottavio *tells Anna* that he will follow her to share in her sorrow, rather than soliloquizing to this effect. More important, this version purports to be modern without becoming a twentieth-century streamlined adaptation. Thus, a typical rendering is "I'm dying" where the original has "From my throbbing breast I feel my soul departing." From what we know of Da Ponte's habits, he would have been the last to object to these changes. He was a businesslike stage writer who patched and shuffled and let others patch and shuffle —it is said that Casanova touched up the text at the last moment—as the performance required.

TEXT

Il dissoluto punito ossia il Don Giovanni in *W. A. Mozart; Werke,* Series 5, No. 18. Leipzig: Breitkopf u. Härtel, in the reproduction of J. W. Edwards, Ann Arbor, Michigan: 1955.

Characters

Don Giovanni	Donna Elvira
Donna Anna	Leporello
Ottavio	Masetto
The Commander	Zerlina

Peasants, Servants, Musicians

Synopsis of Scenes

Act I

1. A garden outside the Commander's palace.
2. A street.
3. The countryside near Don Giovanni's palace.
4. Don Giovanni's garden.
5. A ballroom in Don Giovanni's palace.

Act II

1. A street near Donna Elvira's house.
2. A courtyard in Donna Anna's house.
3. A cemetery.
4. A room in Donna Anna's house.
5. A room in Don Giovanni's house.

Place: A Spanish city

ACT I

Scene 1

A garden. On one side the Commander's palace. In front of it, stone benches. Night. LEPORELLO *is on stage.*

LEPORELLO: I must labor day and night, endure the rain and the wind, eat badly and sleep worse, for a man who knows no gratitude. I'd like to act the gentleman myself, and give up the servant's life. My good master is inside with a pretty girl, needless to say, while I play the sentinel. No, no, I've had enough of serving. Look out! I think somebody's coming. I shouldn't like to be overheard.

[*Enter* ANNA *in pursuit of* DON GIOVANNI.]

ANNA: You won't escape without killing me first!

DON GIOVANNI: Fool! It's no use crying. You'll never know who I am.

LEPORELLO: Oh God, such an uproar, such shouting; my master's in trouble again.

ANNA: People! Servants! Kill the traitor!

DON GIOVANNI: Quiet. Don't infuriate me, or you'll regret it.

ANNA: Scoundrel!

DON GIOVANNI: Stupid woman!

ANNA: I'll hunt you down like a fury.

DON GIOVANNI: This raging woman is bent on destroying me.

LEPORELLO: Let's see if the rascal will ruin me too.

[*The* COMMANDER *rushes in.*]

COMMANDER: Let her go, villain, and draw.

[ANNA, *hearing the Commander, enters the house.*]

DON GIOVANNI: Ha, I wouldn't lower myself.

COMMANDER: Is that how you think you'll get away? Fight!

LEPORELLO [*Aside.*]: If I could only escape.

DON GIOVANNI: Imbecile! Wait, if you want to die.

[*They fight.*]

COMMANDER: Help, I'm betrayed! The murderer has struck me down; I'm dying.

LEPORELLO: Another outrage. I'm half dead with fear. I don't know what to do or say.

DON GIOVANNI: The fool is dead. [*Softly*] Leporello, where are you?

LEPORELLO: Here, unfortunately. And you?

DON GIOVANNI: Here.

LEPORELLO: Who is dead? You or the old man?

DON GIOVANNI: Stupid! The old man.

LEPORELLO: Splendid. Two charming adventures—raping the daughter and killing the father.

DON GIOVANNI: He looked for it.

LEPORELLO: What about Donna Anna?

DON GIOVANNI: Shut your mouth. Don't irritate me, and come along unless you want a taste of something too.

LEPORELLO: I don't want a thing, sir, and my mouth is shut.

[*Exeunt. Enter* ANNA, OTTAVIO, *and servants carrying lights.*]

ANNA: My father's in danger; let's rush to his help!

OTTAVIO: I'll pour out all my blood, if necessary. But where is the ruffian?

ANNA: He's here. Oh God, what do I see? Horrible—Father, Father!

OTTAVIO: Sir—

ANNA: The murderer killed him! Blood—this wound—his pale dead face—no more breath—his limbs cold. Father, my father, my dear! I'm dying—

OTTAVIO: Help her, my friends. Hurry. Bring salts. Anna, my love, my friend! Grief is killing the poor girl.

ANNA: Oh!

OTTAVIO: She's reviving. Let her breathe this again.

ANNA: Father—

OTTAVIO: Remove the body from her eyes. Hide the horrible thing. Dear soul, courage, be comforted.

[*The Commander's body is removed.*]

ANNA: Leave me, cruel man! Let me die too now that my father who gave me life is dead.

OTTAVIO: Listen to me, I beg you. Look at me one quick moment. Look at your lover, who lives only for you.

ANNA: You are—forgive me—my dear—the pain—the anguish—oh— Where is my father?

OTTAVIO: Your father — Dearest, don't remind yourself. In me you will have both husband and father.

ANNA: Swear to avenge this blood if you can!

OTTAVIO: I swear it by your eyes. I swear it by our love.

ANNA: A solemn oath! Fearful moment; I feel a hundred storms in my heart.

[*Exeunt.*]

Scene 2

A street in daylight. Enter DON GIOVANNI *and* LEPORELLO.

DON GIOVANNI: Hurry up. What do you want?

LEPORELLO: It's a matter of some importance.

DON GIOVANNI: Undoubtedly.

LEPORELLO: Of extreme importance, in fact.

DON GIOVANNI: Even better. Get it over with.

LEPORELLO: But swear you won't lose your temper.

DON GIOVANNI: I swear on my honor, provided you don't refer to the Commander.

LEPORELLO: Are we alone?

DON GIOVANNI: As you can see.

LEPORELLO: Nobody overhears us?

DON GIOVANNI: On with it!

LEPORELLO: May I speak quite freely?

DON GIOVANNI: Quite.

LEPORELLO: Well, if that's how it is, my dear lord and master, you are leading the life of a ruffian.

DON GIOVANNI: How dare you—

LEPORELLO: And your oath?

DON GIOVANNI: Hang my oath! Shut your mouth, or else—

LEPORELLO: I won't say a word; I won't breathe, dear master.

DON GIOVANNI: Good; now we're friends. Listen to me. Do you know why we're here?

LEPORELLO: I don't know a thing. But since it's almost day, wouldn't it be a new conquest? I have to know in order to enter it in the list.

DON GIOVANNI: You're a statesman. Know then that I am in love with a beauty, and that I'm sure she loves me. I saw her; spoke with her; and tonight she is coming to the Casino with me. [*Suddenly*] Be still. I smell woman.

LEPORELLO: Gad! Quite an olfactory system!

DON GIOVANNI: At first glance she looks beautiful.

LEPORELLO: Good vision too.

DON GIOVANNI: Let's withdraw and plot our course.

LEPORELLO: He's on fire already.

[*Enter* ELVIRA *in traveling clothes.*]

ELVIRA: Oh who will tell me where that monster is, whom I loved to my disgrace and who betrayed me? If I find him, and if he won't return to me, oh, I'll tear out his heart!

DON GIOVANNI [*to Leporello*]: Did you hear that? A charming girl abandoned by her lover. Poor little thing. Let's try to assuage her torment.

LEPORELLO: That's how he has assuaged a thousand eight hundred others.

DON GIOVANNI: Young lady! Young lady!

ELVIRA: Who is it?

DON GIOVANNI: Good heavens, what do I see?

LEPORELLO: Lovely! It's Elvira.

ELVIRA: Don Giovanni, you here! Ogre, blackguard, miscreant!

LEPORELLO: That's what I call literature! Anyway, she knows her man.

DON GIOVANNI: Now now, dear Elvira, calm down a little and let me speak.

ELVIRA: What can you tell me after such an outrage? You gain entrance into my house by stealth, you succeed in ravishing my heart by means of tricks, oaths, and false hopes; I fall in love with you, cruel man! You call me your wife, and then, disobeying the sacred commands of earth and heaven, you depart criminally from Burgos after three days, you abandon me, you fly from me, you leave me a prey to remorse and to tears, the punishment, no doubt, for my excessive love.

LEPORELLO [Aside.]: She talks like a book!

DON GIOVANNI: Oh but I had my reasons. [To LEPORELLO] Isn't it true?

LEPORELLO: It's true, and strong reasons for that matter.

ELVIRA: And what are they, if not your perfidy and your frivolity? But the justice of heaven ordained that I should find you in order to exact its vengeance and mine.

DON GIOVANNI: Come now, be reasonable. [Aside.] She's nothing but trouble. [Aloud.] If you don't believe my own words, you can believe this gentleman.

LEPORELLO [Aside.]: The devil you can!

DON GIOVANNI: Go on—tell her.

LEPORELLO [softly]: What shall I tell her?

DON GIOVANNI [loud]: Yes, of course, tell her everything.
[Exit.]

ELVIRA: Well then, hurry up.

LEPORELLO: Madam—truly—in this world—inasmuch as it might happen sometime—that the square is not a circle—

ELVIRA: Wretch! Are you laughing at my grief? And you— Heavens, the traitor has fled! Miserable me! Where has he gone?

LEPORELLO: Oh, let him go. He isn't worth thinking about.

ELVIRA: The villain deceived and betrayed me—

LEPORELLO: Console yourself! You neither are, nor were, nor will be the first or the last. Look at this rather heavy book; it's crammed with the names of his conquests. Every house, every village, every country has witnessed his amorous ventures. It is a catalogue, dear lady, of the beauties whom my master has loved. I compiled it myself. Look! read it with me. In Italy, six hundred forty; in Germany, two hundred thirty-one. One hundred in France. In Turkey, ninety-one. But in Spain I've entered already a thousand and three! A thousand and three! You'll find, among them, country girls, waitresses, and city girls. We have countesses, duchesses, baronesses, princesses; women of every rank, of every shape, of every age. Blondes he praises for their gentleness; brunettes, for their constancy; grizzled heads, for their sweetness. In winter he likes them chubby; in summer, he likes them skinny. He calls the tall girl majestic and the short girl cuddlesome. He seduces old women for the sheer pleasure of adding them to the list. His greatest appetite is for ripening virgins. But he doesn't care: let her be rich, let her be ugly, let her be beautiful. As long as she wears a skirt, you know what he'll do.
[*Exit.*]

ELVIRA: Is this how the rascal betrayed me? Is this his inhuman reward for my love? But I'll avenge my wrong. I'll find him before he escapes. Only revenge, spite, and anger speak in my breast.
[*Exit.*]

Scene 3

Countryside near Don Giovanni's palace. ZERLINA, MASETTO, *and a chorus of peasants are singing and dancing. Enter* DON GIOVANNI *and* LEPORELLO.

DON GIOVANNI: Thank God, she's gone. Oh look, look at these jolly young things! What beautiful girls!

LEPORELLO: There should be something for me too in this plenty.

DON GIOVANNI: Good day, dear friends. Continue your merriment. Continue your music, good people. Is this a wedding feast?

ZERLINA: Yes, sir, and I am the bride.

DON GIOVANNI: This is comforting. And the groom?

MASETTO: Myself, at your service.

DON GIOVANNI: Good fellow: at my service. This is speaking like a gentleman.

LEPORELLO [*Aside.*]: It takes a husband to talk like that.

ZERLINA: My Masetto has a golden heart.

DON GIOVANNI: So have I, as it happens. Well now, I want us to be
friends. What is your name?

ZERLINA: Zerlina.

DON GIOVANNI: And yours?

MASETTO: Masetto.

DON GIOVANNI: My dear Masetto! My dear Zerlina! I offer you my
protection. Leporello—what are you up to, you monkey?
[LEPORELLO *is flirting with the girls.*]

LEPORELLO: I'm offering my protection too.

DON GIOVANNI: Quick—take these people to my palace at once; let
them have chocolate, coffee, wines, and cold cuts; entertain them all;
show them the garden, the picture gallery, and the rooms. In short,
see that my Masetto is happy. Understood?

LEPORELLO: Understood. [*To the peasants*] Let's go.

MASETTO: Sir!

DON GIOVANNI: What is it?

MASETTO: Zerlina can't stay without me.

LEPORELLO: His Excellency will take your place. He will know how to
play your part.

DON GIOVANNI: Oh, Zerlina is in the hands of a man of honour. Don't
worry; she'll come along with me presently.

ZERLINA: Go on, don't be afraid. I'm in the hands of a man of honour.

MASETTO: And so—?

ZERLINA: And so there's nothing to fear.

MASETTO: And me? By God—

DON GIOVANNI: Here now, let's stop arguing. If you don't leave without another word, Masetto, watch out, you'll regret it.

MASETTO: I catch on, my lord. I bow my head and I go. Since this is
how you want it, I say no more. You're a man of honour indeed; I
cannot doubt it. Your kindness to me proves it. [*To Zerlina*] You
hussy, you baggage, you always were my undoing. [*To Leporello*]
I'm coming, I'm coming! [*To Zerlina*] You can stay; very respectable
indeed—let my lord make a lady out of you!
[*Exeunt* MASETTO, LEPORELLO, *and peasants.*]

DON GIOVANNI: At last, sweet Zerlinetta, we're rid of that bumpkin.
Did you see me clear the landscape, my love?

ZERLINA: He is my husband, sir.

DON GIOVANNI: Who? That fellow? Do you think that a respectable man, a man of breeding—as I can boast I am—can endure that this sweet, precious face should be pawed by a clodhopper?

ZERLINA: But, sir, I promised to marry him.

DON GIOVANNI: Such promises aren't worth a bean. You're not made to be a farm girl. These roguish eyes, these lovely lips, these white and fragrant little fingers will lead you to a higher station in life. What softness! What perfume!

ZERLINA: I'd rather not.

DON GIOVANNI: What would you rather not?

ZERLINA: Be fooled in the end. I know that you gentlemen are seldom honest and sincere with women.

DON GIOVANNI: This is plebeian propaganda. The honesty of a noble-man is written in his eyes. Well, let's not waste time. I mean to marry you on the spot.

ZERLINA: You?

DON GIOVANNI: Of course. That little house over there is mine: there we'll be alone, my jewel, and there we'll marry; there we'll join hands; there you'll say "I do." Look, it isn't far. Let's leave this place, my love.

ZERLINA [Aside.]: I want to; and then I don't. My heart's in a flutter. It's true I would be happy; but still he might make a fool of me.

DON GIOVANNI: Come, my delight, and soothe the pains of my inno-cent love.

ZERLINA: I'm sorry for Masetto.

DON GIOVANNI: Your life will begin anew.

ZERLINA: I'm weakening. Let's hurry.

DON GIOVANNI: Come!

ZERLINA: Yes.

[Enter ELVIRA.]

ELVIRA: Stop, scoundrel! Heaven has allowed me to overhear your designs. I've come in time to save this poor, innocent wretch from your barbarous claws.

ZERLINA: Poor me! What do I hear?

DON GIOVANNI [Aside.]: Cupid, inspire me. [To Elvira] My queen, don't you see I was only toying?

ELVIRA: Toying! Is that right? Toying! I know, fiend, how you toy.

ZERLINA: Is what she says true, my lord?

DON GIOVANNI [Aside to Elvira.]: The unhappy girl is in love with me and out of pure pity I'm making believe I love her in return. It is my misfortune to have a kind heart.

ELVIRA: Run from the traitor; don't let him speak; his lips lie and his eyes deceive. Trust a woman who suffers and learn from me to beware of this man.

[*Exeunt* ELVIRA *and* ZERLINA.]

DON GIOVANNI: The devil is enjoying himself at my expense today, spoiling all my delightful schemes. Everything is going wrong.

[*Enter* OTTAVIO *and* ANNA.]

OTTAVIO: Henceforth, my treasure, tears are useless. Our theme is vengeance. Oh, Don Giovanni!

DON GIOVANNI [*Aside.*]: That's all I needed!

ANNA: My friend, we have met you in good time. Are you generous and courageous?

DON GIOVANNI [*Aside.*]: Let's see if the devil has told her something. [*Aloud.*]: What a question. Why do you ask?

ANNA: We need your friendship.

DON GIOVANNI [*Aside.*]: I'm breathing again. [*Aloud.*] Command me! Friends, relations, this hand, this blade, my possessions, my blood— I will spend all to serve you. But my beautiful Anna, why are you crying? Who has dared disturb your peace?

[*Enter* ELVIRA.]

ELVIRA [*to Don Giovanni*]: So I find you again, perfidious monster. [*To Anna*] Wretched woman, don't trust this lecher. He has betrayed me and he'll betray you too.

OTTAVIO [*to Anna*]: Heavens, what nobility in her eyes; what sweet dignity.

ANNA [*to Ottavio*]: Her grief and her tears fill me with pity.

DON GIOVANNI: The poor girl is mad, my friends. Leave me with her. I'll calm her down.

ELVIRA: Don't believe the liar!

DON GIOVANNI: She's mad. Please go away!

ELVIRA: Please stay!

ANNA [*to Ottavio*]: Whom should we believe?

OTTAVIO: I'll not leave without seeing clear in this muddle.

ANNA: She looks quite sane to me.

DON GIOVANNI [*Aside.*]: If I leave they'll suspect something.

ELVIRA: You can read his character in his ugly face!

OTTAVIO [*to Don Giovanni*]: So the girl—

DON GIOVANNI: Is not all there.

ANNA [*to Elvira*]: And so you say—

ELVIRA: He's a fraud!

DON GIOVANNI: Unhappy girl!

ELVIRA: Liar!

ANNA [to Ottavio]: I don't know what to believe.

DON GIOVANNI [to Elvira]: Do lower your voice; you're drawing a crowd and exposing your reputation.

ELVIRA: I don't care. I've thrown caution to the winds. The whole world will ring to your guilt and my misery!
  [Exit.]

ANNA [to Ottavio]: This whispering of his, this changing of color— My mind is made up!

DON GIOVANNI: Poor girl! I'd better follow her. Who knows what she might do to herself. Allow me to leave you, beautiful Anna; call on me at home if I can be of any assistance. My friends, good-bye.
  [Exit.]

ANNA: Ottavio, I'm dying.

OTTAVIO: What's the matter?

ANNA: Help me.

OTTAVIO: Courage, my love.

ANNA: Oh God! This is the man who murdered my father!

OTTAVIO: What are you saying?

ANNA: No doubt about it! The last words of that scoundrel—his voice recalled the murderer who entered my room—

OTTAVIO: Is it possible that under the sacred cloak of friendship—but tell me again what happened that night.

ANNA: I was alone in my room late at night when I saw a man come in, wrapped in a cloak. At first I mistook him for you, but then I saw my mistake.

OTTAVIO: Heavens! Go on!

ANNA: He came up to me quietly and sought to embrace me. I tried to free myself, but he pressed me close to him. I cried out. Nobody came. With one hand he covered my mouth, and with the other he clutched me so hard that I thought I was lost.

OTTAVIO: The scoundrel! And then?

ANNA: My terror so increased my strength that finally by pulling, bending, and twisting I managed to get free of him.

OTTAVIO: Thank God! I'm breathing again!

ANNA: I redoubled my cries for help until he fled. I ran boldly into the street to stop him. From defense, I leaped to the attack. My poor old father came running and tried to unmask him, but the ruffian was too strong and killed him. Now you know who tried to dishonour me and who deprived me of my father. If your anger needs reviving, remember the wound in his breast and the ground soaked with his blood.

[*Exit.*]

OTTAVIO: Should I believe that a nobleman can commit such a crime? I must use every means to discover the truth. The duty of a husband and a friend speak in my breast. I must undeceive her or avenge her, for my peace depends on hers. Whatever pleases her gives me life, and whatever grieves her, death.

[*Exit.*]

[*Enter* LEPORELLO.]

LEPORELLO: Happen what may, I must break with this madman. Here he comes. Look at his nonchalance.

[*Enter* DON GIOVANNI.]

DON GIOVANNI: My sweet little Leporello, is everything all right?

LEPORELLO: My sweet little Don Giovanni, everything is all wrong.

DON GIOVANNI: What do you mean, all wrong?

LEPORELLO: I obeyed your orders and took all those people into the house.

DON GIOVANNI: Good.

LEPORELLO: I tried to entertain them with the chatter, the jokes, and the lies I've learned from you.

DON GIOVANNI: Good.

LEPORELLO: I told Masetto a thousand stories to take his mind off his jealousy.

DON GIOVANNI: Excellent.

LEPORELLO: I poured the drinks until they were all half drunk. Some were singing, some were joking, and some just drank. In the middle of which, guess who tumbles in?

DON GIOVANNI: Zerlina.

LEPORELLO: Bravo. And who is with her?

DON GIOVANNI: Elvira.

LEPORELLO: Bravo again. And she spoke of you—

DON GIOVANNI: All the evil she could think of.

LEPORELLO: You are a genius.

DON GIOVANNI: And you, what did you do?

LEPORELLO: Nothing.

DON GIOVANNI: And she?

LEPORELLO: Went on shouting.

DON GIOVANNI: And you?

LEPORELLO: When I judged that she had relieved her feelings, I led her gently out of the garden and, locking the door behind her, cunningly left her alone on the road.

DON GIOVANNI: Masterfully done. Things couldn't be better. Well, I'll finish what you started. These little country girls fascinate me. I want to entertain them till nightfall. Keep the feast going. Make their heads swim in wine. If you find a pretty girl in the square, invite her along. There must be disorder in the dancing. Let one do a minuet, another a fandango, another a jig. And I, meantime, will squeeze one here and kiss one there. By tomorrow, I want another dozen on my list.

[*Exeunt.*]

Scene 4

Don Giovanni's garden. The palace in the back, lit up. Peasants asleep or sitting on the grass. Enter ZERLINA *and* MASETTO.

ZERLINA: Masetto, listen to me. Masetto, I say.

MASETTO: Don't touch me.

ZERLINA: Why not?

MASETTO: Why do you ask? Hussy! I won't stand for your tricks.

ZERLINA: Hush. I don't deserve to be treated so cruelly.

MASETTO: What! You have the cheek to excuse yourself? You stay alone with a man; you jilt me on my wedding day; you shame the honour of a peasant! Oh if it weren't for the scandal, I'd like—

ZERLINA: But if I'm innocent, if he lied to me? What are you afraid of? Calm down, my sweet, he didn't even touch my fingertips. Ungrateful boy, don't you believe me? Come here, vent your anger on me, kill me, do with me what you will, but when you're done, dearest Masetto, when you're done, do let's make up. Beat me, my handsome Masetto, beat your poor Zerlina; I'll be here waiting for your blows as meekly as a little lamb. I'll let you pull my hair out and scratch out my eyes too, and I'll kiss your dear hands. But I see you haven't the heart to do it; so let's make peace, and be merry together night and day.

MASETTO: Look how this witch bamboozles me. We men are weak in the head.

DON GIOVANNI [*within*]: Make everything ready for the feast!

ZERLINA: Masetto, do you hear Monsoor Giovanni's voice?

MASETTO: What's that to me?

ZERLINA: He's coming.

MASETTO: Let him come.

ZERLINA: If I could find a hole to hide in—

MASETTO: What are you afraid of? Why is your face white? Oh, I understand, you hussy; you're afraid I might discover what happened between you two. Quick, before he comes I'm going to disappear. Here's a nook from which I can keep an eye on you.

ZERLINA: Where are you going? Don't hide. Poor boy, what will he do if he finds you?

MASETTO: Let him do or say whatever he likes.

ZERLINA: Words won't help you.

MASETTO: Stand here and speak loud enough for me to hear.

ZERLINA: If that isn't silly!

MASETTO [*Aside*.]: I'll know whether she is faithful and what took place between them.

ZERLINA: The ungrateful and cruel man is upsetting everything today.

[*Enter* DON GIOVANNI *and servants*.]

DON GIOVANNI: Wake up, my good people. There will be pleasure and laughter for all. [*To the servants*] Take them to the ballroom, and let there be plenty of refreshments.

[*Peasants and servants leave*.]

ZERLINA: Maybe he won't see me behind this tree.

DON GIOVANNI: Zerlinetta dear, I see you, you can't escape.

ZERLINA: Let me go.

DON GIOVANNI: No, no, stay, delightful girl.

ZERLINA: Is there no pity in your heart?

DON GIOVANNI: Of course there is, I'm all love. Come with me, you'll be glad if you do.

[*He leads* ZERLINA *toward the place where Masetto is concealed*.]

ZERLINA [*Aside*.]: If he sees Masetto, I know what he's capable of.

DON GIOVANNI: Masetto!

MASETTO: Yes, Masetto.

DON GIOVANNI: Why hidden? Your beautiful Zerlina can't bear to be without you.

MASETTO: I understand, sir.

DON GIOVANNI: Come, cheer up; let's go hear the musicians together.

ZERLINA: Yes, let's cheer up, and let's all three go dancing with the others.

[*Exeunt. Enter* ANNA, ELVIRA, *and* OTTAVIO, *masked.*]

ELVIRA: My friends, with a little courage we shall expose his wickedness.

OTTAVIO: Our friend is right. We need courage. My dear, put away your grief and fear.

ANNA: We're taking a dangerous step. Who knows what complications will follow? I fear for all of us.

LEPORELLO [*from the window*]: My lord, come and see the elegant masqueraders.

DON GIOVANNI: Invite them in and tell them that their presence will honor us.

ANNA: His face and his voice give the traitor away.

LEPORELLO: Pst! You—the maskers!

ANNA: Answer him.

OTTAVIO: What do you want?

LEPORELLO: My master invites you to our ball.

OTTAVIO: Thank you for the courtesy. Let's go, dear ladies.

LEPORELLO [*Aside.*]: Here are two more hens for Master Fox.

ELVIRA: God protect us.

Scene 5

An illuminated ballroom in DON GIOVANNI's *palace. Enter* DON GIOVANNI, LEPORELLO, ZERLINA, *and* MASETTO.

DON GIOVANNI: Rest a little, dear girls.

LEPORELLO: Drink, drink, my lads.

DON GIOVANNI: We'll be frolicking again in a moment. Coffee here!

LEPORELLO: Chocolate!

MASETTO: Zerlina, be careful.

DON GIOVANNI: Sherbets!

LEPORELLO: Sweets!

MASETTO: The scene opens too sweetly. It might turn bitter at the end.

DON GIOVANNI: You are lovely, brilliant, Zerlina!

ZERLINA: You're too kind.

MASETTO [*Aside.*]: The hussy is eating it up.

LEPORELLO: Sweet Gianotta, charming Sandrina!

MASETTO [*Aside.*]: Go on—touch her, and the devil take you.

ZERLINA [*Aside.*]: Masetto seems to be in a rage. How very unpleasant.

DON GIOVANNI [*Aside.*]: Masetto seems to be in a rage. This calls for brainwork.

Masetto [*Aside.*]: Touch her, touch her! The hussy is driving me mad.
   [*Enter* Anna, Elvira, *and* Ottavio, *masked.*]
Leporello: Come in, pretty maskers!
Don Giovanni: It's open house for all. A toast to liberty!
Ottavio: We are grateful for so many tokens of your generosity.
All Five: Liberty!
Don Giovanni: Let the players strike up again. [*To* Leporello] Pair off the dancers. Zerlina, come here, you must dance with me.
Leporello: Everybody dance.
Elvira: There's the girl.
Anna: I can't bear it.
Ottavio: Dissemble.
Don Giovanni: Everything's running smoothly.
Masetto [*ironically*]: Everything's running ever so smoothly.
Don Giovanni [*to* Leporello]: Keep an eye on Masetto.
Leporello [*to* Masetto]: Aren't you dancing, poor fellow? Come along with me, let's join the others.
Don Giovanni: I'm your partner, Zerlina. Come with me. [*They dance.*]
Masetto: No—I don't want to dance.
Leporello: Yes, you do.
Masetto: No, I don't.
Leporello: We'll do like everybody else.
   [*He dances with* Masetto.]
Anna: I can't hold back.
Ottavio: I beg you, keep still a little longer.
Don Giovanni [*to* Zerlina]: Follow me, my dearest.
Masetto [*to* Leporello]: Let me go! [*To Zerlina*] No! Zerlina!
Don Giovanni: Come, come.
Zerlina: Oh Gods, I'm betrayed!
   [*Dancing,* Don Giovanni *leads* Zerlina *to a door and forces her to enter.*]
Leporello: Here comes trouble.
   [*He runs to warn Don Giovanni.*]
Anna: The scoundrel is walking into the trap by himself.
Zerlina [*within*]: Help! Everybody! Help!
Anna: Let's help the innocent girl!
   [*The musicians, etc., leave in confusion.*]
Masetto: Zerlina!
Zerlina [*within*]: Beast!

ANNA: The cries are coming from that side. Tear down the door.

ZERLINA: Help me! I'll die.

OTTAVIO: We're here to defend you.

[*They force the door.* ZERLINA *appears, followed by* DON GIOVANNI, *who, sword in hand, is dragging* LEPORELLO *along, and pretends to threaten him.*]

DON GIOVANNI: Here's the villain who molested you; but I'll punish him. Die, miserable wretch.

LEPORELLO: What are you doing?

DON GIOVANNI: I said, die.

OTTAVIO [*pistol in hand, removes his mask*]: Stop! We've seen through your tricks.

[ANNA *and* ELVIRA *take off their masks.*]

DON GIOVANNI: Elvira!

ELVIRA: Yes, you devil.

DON GIOVANNI: Ottavio!

OTTAVIO: Yes.

DON GIOVANNI [*to Anna*]: Believe me—

OTTAVIO: Everything is known.

ELVIRA: Tremble, rascal. The whole world will know your crimes and your cruelties.

ANNA: Listen to the thunder of vengeance crashing about you. The bolt will fall on your head today.

LEPORELLO: My head's in a whirl; what a horrible storm!

DON GIOVANNI: Do you take me for a coward? I defy you all! If the world itself came down on me, I wouldn't shake.

[*He escapes.*]

ACT II

Scene 1

A street. On one side Donna Elvira's house, with a balcony. Night. Enter DON GIOVANNI *and* LEPORELLO.

DON GIOVANNI: Come on, you clown, don't pester me.

LEPORELLO: Well, I won't stay with you.

DON GIOVANNI: Look here, my friend—

LEPORELLO: I'm leaving, I tell you.

DON GIOVANNI: What have I done to you?

LEPORELLO: Oh nothing at all; just nearly killed me.

DON GIOVANNI: You're a fool. That was only a joke.

LEPORELLO: Well, I'm not joking, and I'm leaving.

DON GIOVANNI: Leporello.

LEPORELLO: Sir?

DON GIOVANNI: Come here. Let's make up. Take this.

LEPORELLO: What is it?

DON GIOVANNI: Four ducats.

LEPORELLO: Well— I'm playing along with this ceremony one more time; but don't get used to it; don't think you can bedevil the likes of me with money, the way you do your women.

DON GIOVANNI: Let's say no more about it. Have you got courage enough to carry out my orders?

LEPORELLO: Provided there are no women in it.

DON GIOVANNI: No women? Idiot! No women! Do you realize that they are more necessary to me than breathing and eating?

LEPORELLO: And in spite of that you keep on cheating them?

DON GIOVANNI: It's all for the sake of love. He who serves one woman only, robs every other. And such is the tenderness of my emotions that I adore them all. Unfortunately women have no common sense and call my good nature treachery.

LEPORELLO: I've never seen a more extensive good nature. Well—what do you want now?

DON GIOVANNI: Listen. Have you seen Elvira's maid?

LEPORELLO: I haven't.

DON GIOVANNI: In that case, my dear Leporello, you have missed a beautiful object. I'm going to try my luck with her. And since it's almost night, I've decided to appear in your clothes in order to sharpen her appetite.

LEPORELLO: Why don't you appear in your own?

DON GIOVANNI: People of her class are suspicious of elegant dress. Well now, hurry up.

LEPORELLO: Sir—I don't feel—

DON GIOVANNI [angry]: Enough. I can't bear objections. [They exchange cloaks. ELVIRA appears at the balcony.]

ELVIRA: Be still, my heart. He is a cruel traitor. To feel for him is a sin.

LEPORELLO: Hush. I hear Donna Elvira's voice.

DON GIOVANNI: I'm going to take advantage of this. Stand here. Elvira, my treasure!

ELVIRA: Isn't that the ingrate speaking?

DON GIOVANNI: Yes, my life, it is I, begging your forgiveness.

ELVIRA [*Aside.*]: Gods, what a strange feeling he wakes in my breast!

LEPORELLO [*Aside.*]: You'll see how that madwoman will still believe him.

DON GIOVANNI: Come down, joy of my life. You're the one my soul adores. I've already repented.

ELVIRA: No, villain, I don't believe you.

DON GIOVANNI: Believe me, or I will kill myself!

LEPORELLO: If you go on I'm going to laugh.

DON GIOVANNI: Come down, my goddess.

ELVIRA [*Aside.*]: Oh, I'm struggling with myself. Shall I go? Shall I stay? God protect a poor gullible woman!

DON GIOVANNI [*Aside.*]: I hope she falls for this. It's a neat little trick. Was there ever a greater talent than mine?

LEPORELLO [*Aside.*]: The liar is seducing her again. God protect the fool!

[ELVIRA *withdraws from the balcony.*]

DON GIOVANNI: Well, what do you think?

LEPORELLO: I think you have a heart of stone.

DON GIOVANNI: You're a big simpleton. Now listen— When she comes down, take her in your arms, pat her a few times, and imitate my voice. Then use your wits to take her away from here.

LEPORELLO: But—

DON GIOVANNI: Don't answer.

LEPORELLO: And if she recognizes me?

DON GIOVANNI: She won't if you don't want her to. Quiet, she's coming; use your head!

[DON GIOVANNI *conceals himself; enter* ELVIRA.]

ELVIRA: I've come to you.

DON GIOVANNI [*Aside.*]: Let's see what he does.

LEPORELLO [*Aside.*]: What a muddle.

ELVIRA: Can I really believe that my tears have overcome your heart? Is my dear Giovanni returning to his duty and to my love?

LEPORELLO: Yes, my darling.

ELVIRA: Cruel man! If you knew how many tears and sighs I've spent on you!

LEPORELLO: On me?

ELVIRA: Yes, you.

LEPORELLO: Poor dear, I'm so sorry.

ELVIRA: You'll never leave me again?

LEPORELLO: No, sweetie.

ELVIRA: Will you always be mine?

LEPORELLO: Always.

ELVIRA: Dearest.

LEPORELLO: Dearest. [*Aside.*] I'm beginning to enjoy this.

ELVIRA: My treasure!

LEPORELLO: My Venus!

ELVIRA: I'm all fire for you.

LEPORELLO: And I'm burnt to ashes.

DON GIOVANNI [*Aside.*]: The rogue is warming up.

ELVIRA: And you won't betray me?

LEPORELLO: Certainly not.

ELVIRA: Swear it!

LEPORELLO: I swear it to this hand, which I kiss with rapture, and to these two stars—

DON GIOVANNI [*making rough noises*]: You're dead.

ELVIRA and LEPORELLO: Oh! God!

[ELVIRA *and* LEPORELLO *fly.*]

DON GIOVANNI [*laughing*]: Luck is with me. Let's see; these are the windows; now to my song.

[*He sings a serenade.*]

There's someone at the window. Maybe it's she. Pst, pst.

[*Enter* MASETTO, *followed by armed peasants.*]

MASETTO: Let's not give up; I'm sure we'll find him!

DON GIOVANNI [*Aside.*]: Somebody is talking.

MASETTO: Stop! I think somebody's moving there.

DON GIOVANNI [*Aside.*]: If I'm not mistaken it's Masetto.

MASETTO: Who goes there? No answer? Courage; shoulder your muskets. Who goes there?

DON GIOVANNI [*Aside.*]: He's not alone; I've got to be careful. [*Aloud, trying to imitate Leporello's voice*] Friends! [*Aside.*] I don't want to be seen. [*Aloud.*] Is that you, Masetto?

MASETTO: Nobody else, and you?

DON GIOVANNI: Don't you recognize me? Don Giovanni's servant.

MASETTO: Leporello! That scoundrel's servant?

DON GIOVANNI: That's right; the rascal's servant.

MASETTO: Tell me where we can find him. I've a little group here all set to kill him.

DON GIOVANNI [*Aside.*]: A trifle. [*Aloud.*] Excellent. I'm going to join you to get even with that pest of a master. But listen to my sugges-

tion: half of you go one way and half the other. He can't be very far.
If you see a couple walking on the square, or if you hear someone
making declarations under a window, shoot and shoot again; it's
my master. He's wearing a hat with white feathers, a broad cloak,
and a sword at his side. Hurry up men! You alone stay behind with
me. We'll take care of the rest and you'll soon find out what that is.

[*The peasants leave.*]

DON GIOVANNI: All's quiet. Excellent. So we're going to kill him?

MASETTO: That's right.

DON GIOVANNI: You wouldn't be satisfied just to break his bones, or
maybe to knock in a rib or two?

MASETTO: No, I want to kill him and make mincemeat of him.

DON GIOVANNI: Do you have good weapons?

MASETTO: Yes, by thunder. First I've got this musket; then, this pistol.

[*He gives them to Don Giovanni.*]

DON GIOVANNI: Anything else?

MASETTO: Isn't that enough?

DON GIOVANNI: I suppose it is. Now take this for the pistol, and that
for the musket.

[*Beats him.*]

MASETTO: Ouch, ouch, my head!

DON GIOVANNI: Shut up, or I'll butcher you. Take this for killing him;
and that, for the mincemeat. Ruffian! Cutthroat! Dog!

[*Exit* DON GIOVANNI; *enter* ZERLINA *with a lantern.*]

MASETTO: Oh my head! Oh my shoulders! Oh my chest!

ZERLINA: I thought I heard Masetto's voice.

MASETTO: Oh God, Zerlina, help me.

ZERLINA: What happened?

MASETTO: That devil broke all my bones.

ZERLINA: Goodness! Who was it?

MASETTO: Leporello, or some devil that looks like him.

ZERLINA: Fool! Didn't I tell you that your stupid jealousy would bring
you to grief? Where does it hurt?

MASETTO: Here.

ZERLINA: Where else?

MASETTO: Here; and here.

ZERLINA: And nowhere else?

MASETTO: This foot hurts a little; and this arm; and this hand.

ZERLINA: Well, that's no great matter, if the rest of you is sound. Come
home with me. If you promise to be less jealous in the future, I myself

will take care of you, my dear boy. You'll see what a fine remedy I
have for you. It's a natural cure, it has no bad taste, and it's a thing
the druggist doesn't know how to make. I carry it on me all the time,
and I'll give it to you if you want to try it. Would you like to know
where it is? Feel here. Do you hear it beating? Just put your hand
there. There. There.

[*Exeunt.*]

Scene 2

A dark courtyard in Donna Anna's house. Enter LEPORELLO *and*
ELVIRA.

LEPORELLO: I see torches coming near. Let's stay here a little, my
love, until they disappear.

ELVIRA: What are you afraid of, my beloved husband?

LEPORELLO: Nothing. I want to be careful. I'll go see if the lights are
gone. [*Aside.*] How can I get rid of her? [*Aloud.*] Stay here, my jewel.
[*He moves away.*]

ELVIRA: Don't leave me alone in this darkness. My heart is beating so.
I'll die of fear.
[*Groping about.*]

LEPORELLO [*Aside.*]: The more I look for that miserable door, the less
I find it. Softly, I have it! Now's the time to escape. [*He misses the
door. Enter* OTTAVIO *and* ANNA *with torches.*]

OTTAVIO: Dry your tears, dearest, and soothe your grief. Your father's
shade will take pity on your suffering from now on.

ANNA: These tears are my only relief— Don't forbid me to weep. Only
death can dry my eyes.

ELVIRA [*Aside.*]: Where is my husband?

LEPORELLO [*Aside.*]: If she finds me, I'm done for.

ELVIRA: Here's a door. I'll leave quietly.
[*Enter* ZERLINA *and* MASETTO.]

MASETTO: Stop, villain; where are you going?

OTTAVIO: Here's the traitor. What was he doing here?

ANNA: Kill the scoundrel who wronged me.

ELVIRA: He's my husband. Mercy! Forgive him!

ANNA: Donna Elvira! I can hardly believe it.

OTTAVIO: Let him die.
[*He is about to kill* LEPORELLO.]

ELVIRA: Mercy!

LEPORELLO [*on his knees*]: Mercy, mercy, my lords. I'm not him; she's mistaken. Let me live, for pity's sake.

ALL: It's Leporello— What trick is this? I'm dumbfounded— What does this mean?

LEPORELLO: It'll be a miracle if I can save my skin this time.

[ANNA *leaves.*]

ZERLINA: So you're the one who was mauling my Masetto just now.

ELVIRA: So you're the one who duped me playing Don Giovanni with me.

OTTAVIO: So you came disguised to make fools of us.

ELVIRA: His punishment is reserved to me.

ZERLINA: No, to me.

OTTAVIO: No, no, to me.

MASETTO: ~~The three of you join me in~~ beating him up.

LEPORELLO: Mercy, mercy, my lords and ladies. I can explain everything. The crime's not my own. My master robbed me of my innocence. Donna Elvira, pity me—you know what happened. And you can bear witness that I don't know a thing about Masetto. I've been walking about with you for about an hour. [*To* OTTAVIO] To you, dear sir, I don't say anything. I was scared—as luck would have it— light outside—dark here—no way out—the door—the wall—I went to that side—I took cover—I'm sure you understand—but if I'd known —I would have—cleared out!

[*Runs away.*]

ELVIRA: Stop! Stop!

MASETTO: The dog has wings at his feet.

ZERLINA: How cleverly he escaped.

OTTAVIO: Friends: After such egregious crimes, we can no longer hesitate to call Don Giovanni the impious assassin of Donna Anna's father. Remain a few hours in this house. I shall call in the constables, and soon you will all be revenged. So much is required of duty, pity, and love. Meanwhile, go and comfort my bride; wipe her precious tears; tell her I have gone to avenge her wrongs, and that I shall return only with a message of death and destruction.

[*Exeunt all except* ELVIRA.]

ELVIRA: He betrays me, he abandons me, he covers himself with crimes, he calls down on his head the justice of heaven, and yet I pity him. I clamor for vengeance—and then my heart speaks for him. Oh, unhappy girl!

[*Exit* ELVIRA.]

Scene 3

A cemetery surrounded by a wall. Among other statues, that of the COMMANDER *on horseback. Moonlight. Enter* DON GIOVANNI, *climbing down the wall.*

DON GIOVANNI [*laughing*]: That was delicious; now let her find me. What a beautiful night; brighter than the day. It seems made to roam after pretty girls. Is it late? No; not even two. I wonder how the business of Leporello and Elvira ended. I hope he didn't lose his head.

LEPORELLO [*outside the gate*]: He'll be the death of me at last.

DON GIOVANNI: That's him. Hey, Leporello!

LEPORELLO: Who's calling me?

DON GIOVANNI: Don't you know your master?

LEPORELLO: I wish I didn't.

DON GIOVANNI: What's that, you cur?

LEPORELLO: Oh, it's you. Excuse me.

DON GIOVANNI: What happened?

LEPORELLO: I was almost killed on your account.

DON GIOVANNI: Well, wasn't that an honour for you?

LEPORELLO: The honour's all yours.

DON GIOVANNI: Come here; I've a few lovely things to tell you.

LEPORELLO: What are you doing here?

DON GIOVANNI: Come here, and you'll find out. I've had a dozen adventures since I last saw you. But those can wait; just listen to the best one of the lot.

LEPORELLO: Romantic, of course.

DON GIOVANNI: Can you doubt it? I met a beautiful, young, and sprightly girl in the street. I followed her. I took her hand. She tried to run away. I said a few words, and she mistook me for—guess whom?

LEPORELLO: I don't know.

DON GIOVANNI: For Leporello.

LEPORELLO: For me?

DON GIOVANNI: For you.

LEPORELLO: Fine.

DON GIOVANNI: She takes me by the hand.

LEPORELLO: Still better.

DON GIOVANNI: She fondles me, she kisses me. "My dear Leporello. My sweet Leporello." I realized that she was one of your mistresses.

LEPORELLO [*Aside.*]: Damn him.

DON GIOVANNI: I took advantage of her mistake, but finally she recognized me. She began to shout; I heard people and started running. I ran until I came to this wall, jumped over it like a cat, and landed here.

LEPORELLO: And you tell me all this so lightly?

DON GIOVANNI: Why not?

LEPORELLO: Suppose it had been my wife?

DON GIOVANNI [*laughing*]: Better still.

STATUE: Before dawn your laughter will cease.

DON GIOVANNI: Who spoke?

LEPORELLO: It must be a soul from the other world that knows you thoroughly.

DON GIOVANNI: Quiet, fool. Who goes there?

[*He searches the cemetery, striking several statues with his sword.*]

STATUE: Abandoned wretch, leave the dead in peace.

LEPORELLO: I told you so.

DON GIOVANNI [*disdainful*]: It must be somebody over the wall playing a joke on us. Look! Isn't that the Commander's statue? Read the inscription.

LEPORELLO: Excuse me, but I haven't learned to read by moonlight.

DON GIOVANNI: Read, I tell you.

LEPORELLO: "I wait for vengeance against the villain who murdered me." Did you hear that? I'm shaking like a leaf.

DON GIOVANNI: The old clown! Tell him I expect him for dinner tonight.

LEPORELLO: This is insane. But I think— Good God, do you see the terrible looks he's giving us? He seems to be alive; he looks as though he could hear—as though he wanted to speak.

DON GIOVANNI: Proceed, or I'll carve you up and bury you on the spot.

LEPORELLO: Easy, easy. I'm going. Oh distinguished Statue of the great Commander— My heart's beating too fast, I can't finish.

DON GIOVANNI: Finish, or I'll run you through. [*Aside.*] What a lark! I'll make him sweat.

LEPORELLO [*Aside.*]: I'm stuck with it. My blood's curdling. [*Aloud.*] Distinguished Statue, although you're made of marble— Master, look at him stare!

DON GIOVANNI: Die!

LEPORELLO: Wait! [*to the Statue*] Sir—my master—my master desires to dine with you. Oh, oh, what a sight! Oh heavens, he nodded!

DON GIOVANNI: You're nothing but a clown.

LEPORELLO: Why don't you look?

DON GIOVANNI: What should I look at?

LEPORELLO: He went [*nods*] with his head.

DON GIOVANNI [*to the Statue*]: Speak if you can. Will you dine with me?

STATUE: Yes.

LEPORELLO: I can't move; I can't breathe. For pity's sake, let's get out of here.

DON GIOVANNI: It's a strange affair, to be sure. The old man's coming to dinner. Well, a meal has to be prepared, so let's be off.
[*Exeunt.*]

Scene 4

A room in Donna Anna's house. Lights on the tables. Enter ANNA *and* OTTAVIO.

OTTAVIO: Calm yourself, my treasure; soon we shall see the excesses of that villain punished.

ANNA: But my father—

OTTAVIO: We must bow to the will of God. Dearest, if tomorrow you should wish to find compensation for your bitter loss—this heart, this hand, which my tender love—

ANNA: Oh God, what are you saying, at a time like this?

OTTAVIO: Will you increase my grief with new delays? Cruel love!

ANNA: Not cruel, dearest. It grieves me too to defer what both our souls desire. But what would the world say? Don't tempt me. You know that love pleads for you; you know my constancy. Don't torment yourself, unless you wish me to die. Perhaps some day Heaven will pity me.

OTTAVIO: Let me go with you and share in your sorrows.
[*Exeunt.*]

Scene 5

A lighted room in Don Giovanni's house. A table is set for dinner. Enter DON GIOVANNI, LEPORELLO, *and musicians.*

DON GIOVANNI: The table is set; play, musicians. I'm spending money and I mean to enjoy myself. Leporello, start serving.

LEPORELLO: I'm ready. Bravo! They're playing "Cosa Rara."

Don Giovanni: What do you think of the music?

Leporello: Worthy of you.

Don Giovanni: A delicious dish.

Leporello [Aside.]: Look at that appetite. Each mouthful would feed a giant. It makes me sick.

Don Giovanni [Aside.]: Leporello looks hungry. Next course!

Leporello: Coming up.

Don Giovanni: Pour the wine.

[The music changes.]

Leporello: Ah! They're playing "I Due Litiganti."

Don Giovanni: Excellent marzimino!

Leporello [Aside.]: I'm going to swallow this chunk of pheasant on the sly.

Don Giovanni [Aside.]: The scamp is eating my dinner. I'll pretend not to notice.

[The music changes to "Non più andrai."]

Leporello: I've heard that one too often.

Don Giovanni: Leporello!

Leporello [with his mouth full]: Sir.

Don Giovanni: Speak clearly, you dog.

Leporello: My cold keeps me from enunciating.

Don Giovanni: Whistle a little while I eat.

Leporello: I can't.

Don Giovanni: What happened?

Leporello: Forgive me. Your cook is so good that I wanted to sample his skill.

[Enter Elvira.]

Elvira: I want to give you a last proof of my love. I have forgotten your deceptions. I feel only pity for you.

Don Giovanni [Aside.]: What now?

[Motions to the musicians to leave.]

Elvira [kneeling]: I ask nothing for myself.

Don Giovanni: I'm astounded! What do you want? If you don't rise, I'll kneel too.

[He kneels.]

Elvira: Don't laugh at my sorrow!

Leporello [Aside.]: I feel like crying.

Don Giovanni [with feigned tenderness]: Me? Laugh at you? Why should I? What do you want, my love?

ELVIRA: Mend your life.

DON GIOVANNI: Good girl.

[*He laughs.*]

ELVIRA: Monster!

DON GIOVANNI: Let me continue with my meal; and join me, if you like.

ELVIRA: No—I'll leave you in the stench of your hateful vices, a horrible example to mankind.

LEPORELLO [*Aside.*]: If he's not moved by this, he has a heart of stone, or none at all.

DON GIOVANNI: Long live women! Long live good wine! The comfort and glory of mankind!

[*On her way out,* ELVIRA *shrieks and departs by another door.*]

DON GIOVANNI: What's this scream? Go see what happened.

[LEPORELLO *leaves, shrieks too, and returns.*]

LEPORELLO: Oh!

DON GIOVANNI: What a fiendish scream! Leporello, what is it?

LEPORELLO: Merciful heavens, don't move! It's the man of stone, the white man. Master, I'm going out of my mind! If you'd seen his shape—if you'd heard how he walks—ta, ta, ta, ta.

DON GIOVANNI: I don't understand a word you're saying. You're out of your head.

LEPORELLO: Listen.

DON GIOVANNI: There's a knock. Open!

LEPORELLO: No.

DON GIOVANNI: Open, I say!

LEPORELLO: Aaah!

DON GIOVANNI: Idiot! I'll have to open myself and clear up this mystery.

[*Takes the light and goes to the door.*]

LEPORELLO: I don't want to see the old boy any more. Where can I hide?

[*He hides under the table.*]

[*Enter* DON GIOVANNI *and the* COMMANDER.]

COMMANDER: Don Giovanni, you invited me to dinner, and I have come.

DON GIOVANNI: I would never have believed it. But I'll do what I can. Leporello, another plate!

LEPORELLO: Master—we're dead.

DON GIOVANNI: Go on, I tell you.

COMMANDER: Stop. He who feasts on heavenly fare requires no mortal food. Graver cares brought me back to the world.

LEPORELLO: I've a fever and can't keep my limbs still.

DON GIOVANNI: Well then, speak! What do you want?

COMMANDER: Listen. My time is short.

DON GIOVANNI: Speak. I'm listening.

COMMANDER: You invited me to dinner. Now you know your duty. Answer me: will you dine with me?

LEPORELLO: Hallo! He's engaged; excuse him.

DON GIOVANNI: I'll never be smirched with the name of coward.

COMMANDER: Decide!

DON GIOVANNI: I have decided.

COMMANDER: Will you come?

LEPORELLO: Say no.

DON GIOVANNI: I stand firm and without fear. I'll come!

COMMANDER: Give me your hand as a pledge.

DON GIOVANNI: Here it is. Ay! His grip is like ice.

COMMANDER: Repent! Mend your life. This is your last chance.

DON GIOVANNI [*tries in vain to free himself*]: No, I do not repent. Let me go! Away!

COMMANDER: Repent, scoundrel!

DON GIOVANNI: Never, old fool!

COMMANDER: Repent!

LEPORELLO: Do.

COMMANDER: Repent!

DON GIOVANNI: No.

COMMANDER: Ah! There's no more time.

[*He vanishes. Fire and thunder.*]

DON GIOVANNI: My mind darkens. The fires of hell surround me. Oh the torment! the delirium! Infernal terror!

INVISIBLE CHORUS: For guilt like yours this is all too little. Come; there's worse below!

DON GIOVANNI: Who is tearing my soul out? Who is burning my flesh?

LEPORELLO: Despair! Terror! Groans! Shouts! Damnation!

[DON GIOVANNI *disappears. Enter* ANNA, ELVIRA, ZERLINA, OTTAVIO, *and* MASETTO.]

OTTAVIO: Where's the villain?

ELVIRA: Where's the wretch?

ANNA: I must see him in chains.

LEPORELLO: You'll never find him. Stop looking. He's gone forever.

ELVIRA: What happened? Speak!

OTTAVIO: Speak up!

LEPORELLO: A giant came—I can't describe him.

MASETTO: Keep talking!

LEPORELLO: There was fire and smoke—wait a bit—a man of stone— don't come nearer—right here—he took the plunge—right here the devil gulped him down.

ALL: Heavens! Can it be true?

LEPORELLO: Yes, it's true.

ELVIRA: It must have been the ghost I saw.

OTTAVIO: Now, dearest, we are all avenged. Dally no more, and make me the happiest of men.

ANNA: Grant me another year of mourning. Be patient and yield to me, my love.

OTTAVIO: I must yield to the woman who adores me.

ELVIRA: And I will end my life in a convent.

ZERLINA: And Masetto and me are going home for dinner.

LEPORELLO: And I'm off to the nearest inn to find a better master.

ALL: Now let the scoundrel stay with Proserpine and Pluto. And let us all, good people, joyously repeat the old, old song: Such is the end of evildoers! The death of villains is always as evil as their lives!